advancing learning, changing lives

Dream

D

Jan
Consul

Edexcel Limited
190 High Holborn
London
WC1V 7BH

Developed from the training material of Symbiosis.

Symbiosis is an accredited Macromedia training provider and offers a number of DiDA-specific training courses. Please see www.symbiosis.com for more details.

Jane McNeill is a director of Symbiosis.

ISBN   1-84690-107-3
        978-1-84690-107-2

Designed by Peter Simmonett

Printed and bound by CPI Bath

The publisher's policy is to use paper manufactured from sustainable forests.

Acknowledgments
The publisher would like to thank many people for their help, support and encouragement in the production of this material, in particular Jenny Gillies and Catherine Taylor.

Every effort has been made to trace and acknowledge ownership of copyright. If any have been overlooked, the publisher will be pleased to make the necessary changes at the earliest opportunity.

Dreamweaver is a trademark of Macromedia.

All trademarks are the property of their respective owners.

Throughout this book trademarks are used. Rather than put a trademark symbol with every occurrence of a trademarked name, we state that we are using the names in an editorial fashion only and to the benefit of the trademark owner with no intention of infringement of copyright. No such use, or the use of any trade name, is intended to convey endorsement or other affiliation with this book.

CONTENTS

1 Using Dreamweaver for DiDA

Why use Dreamweaver?

Dreamweaver is a web authoring tool produced by Macromedia. You can use it to create exciting web pages that can be connected together to make a website.

Using Dreamweaver you can bring together a variety of media to present your message to your audience and you can add interactivity and links to create an exciting publication for your target audience.

Dreamweaver uses a point and click interface that makes most tasks easy. Tasks such as inserting images can all be done using about three mouse clicks. The way that text and images appear on the page is controlled by their properties.

- Text can use different fonts, be different weights, font colours, sizes etc.
- Images can be sized, cropped, linked to other pages etc.
- Movies can be played on the page or opened in other windows.

You find these options in the properties panel:

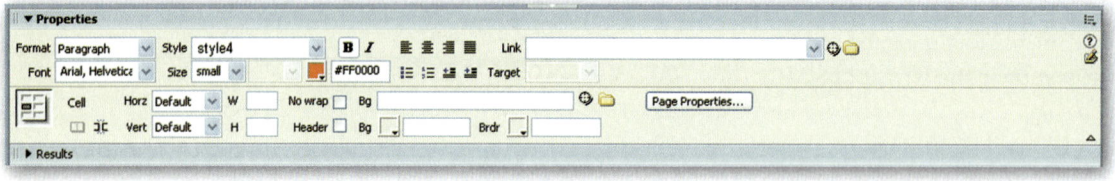

You could write HyperText Markup Language (html) code in Dreamweaver but you also have the option to use the WYSIWYG (What You See Is What You Get) interface.

These are three views of the same page: the first one shows the design view that you will be using as you work through this book; the second view is the html code for the page; and the third view shows the code and the page at the same time.

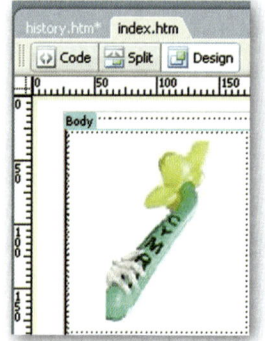
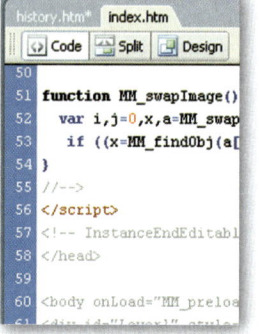
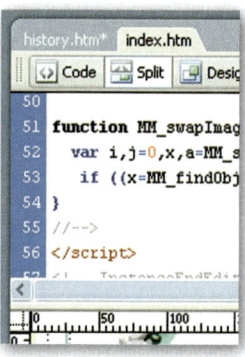

Dreamweaver and DiDA

You can use Dreamweaver in different ways to help you succeed in your DiDA work.

- You can use Dreamweaver to create publications to get your message across to your target audience.
- In Using ICT you can use Dreamweaver to create websites and information points.
- In Multimedia you can use Dreamweaver to make interactive products such as virtual tours, e-learning packages or even e-books.
- In Graphics and Enterprise you can use Dreamweaver to showcase your achievements and enhance the visual experience of your target audience.

You can also use Dreamweaver to create your E-portfolio to showcase your Summative Project Brief work for your teacher and your moderator. This will be you chance to show off all your hard work so it will be very important that your E-portfolio looks good, works well and impresses your audience.

Developing a successful E-portfolio for DiDA

This book helps you develop the skills that you will need if you want to create your E-portfolio in Dreamweaver. The success of your E-portfolio will depend partly on your Dreamweaver skills and partly on the skills you will have developed in your DiDA work.

An E-portfolio is another publication just like any websites or information points you may create as you work through the SPB.

This book has been written to help you produce publications and E-portfolios that will impress your teachers and the moderator. If you follow the instructions in the following chapters you will learn all the skills that you will need to build a good E-portfolio if you choose to use Dreamweaver.

How to use this book

The book has been written to cover all the Dreamweaver skills you might want to use in any of your E-portfolios.

Chapters 2 to 5 show you the useful skills, giving step-by-step guidance. The authors suggest that you work through the chapters in the order given as the skills build up as you go along.

The contents page at the beginning of the book gives an easy reference guide to finding a particular skill.

The Hints and Tips sections provide further information for anyone interested in understanding a little more about how Dreamweaver works.

Using this book to help you do well

The book will give you a chance to practise the skills through your work on the Project from the Edexcel DiDA Using ICT Student Book.

The 'Over to you' sections will suggest how to apply the skills step-by-step in the Food Matters! Project.

This gives you a chance to try out the new skills for yourself so you are sure that you really understood how to use the skills in the real E-portfolio.

You can still use this book if you don't have a copy of the Edexcel DiDA Using ICT book. Use the Over to you sections to apply the skills to the E-portfolio you are building for your own project.

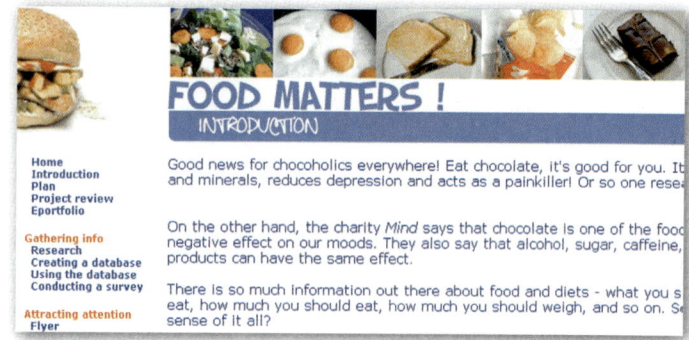

Before you start

As with any other publication, before you start you must ask yourself the following five questions: Who? Why? Where? What? How?

The 'Who?', the target audience, are the people who will assess your work – the teacher and the moderator – and the 'Why?' is because they must decide how successful you have been.

The 'Where?' 'What?' and 'How?' now need to be answered.

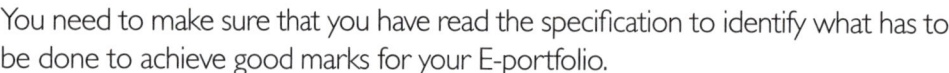

You need to make sure that you have read the specification to identify what has to be done to achieve good marks for your E-portfolio.

The mark descriptions will help you design your prototype portfolio.

As you work through your Food Matters! E-portfolio you will need to use the production cycle that you have seen on page 28 of the Edexcel DiDA Using ICT Student Book.

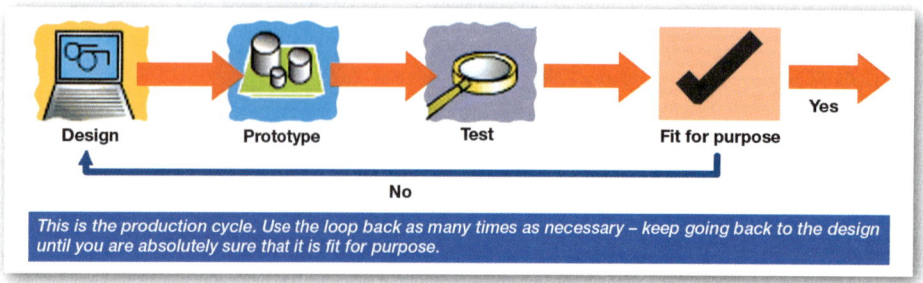

This is the production cycle. Use the loop back as many times as necessary – keep going back to the design until you are absolutely sure that it is fit for purpose.

Remember that your E-portfolio will only succeed if you ask your peers, teacher and test reviewers for feedback that you can use to improve your publication.

2 Getting started

Define your project settings

Before you start to build a website you need to 'Define the Site'. This tells Dreamweaver where the local **Root Folder** that will hold all your files for the site is located and should make sure that everything you use to build the site is held together in one place.

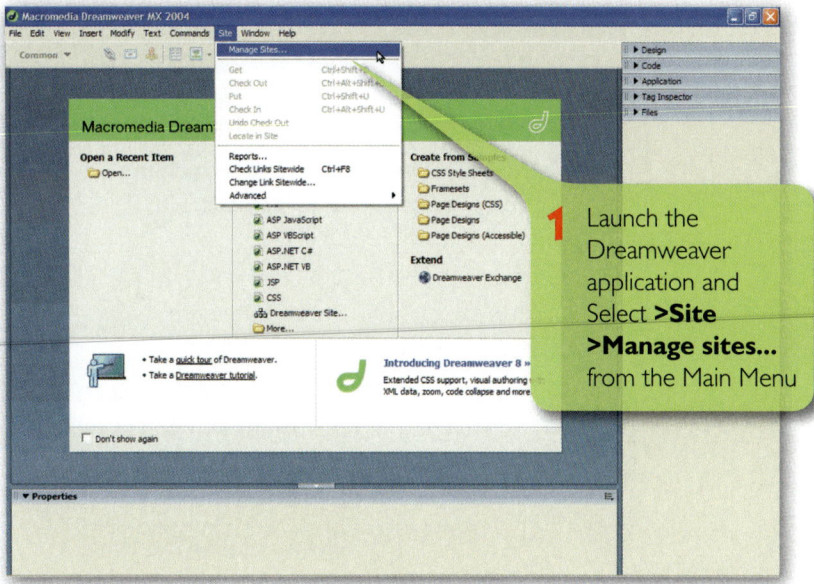

1 Launch the Dreamweaver application and Select **>Site >Manage sites...** from the Main Menu

2 Select **>New** and Choose the **>Site** option.

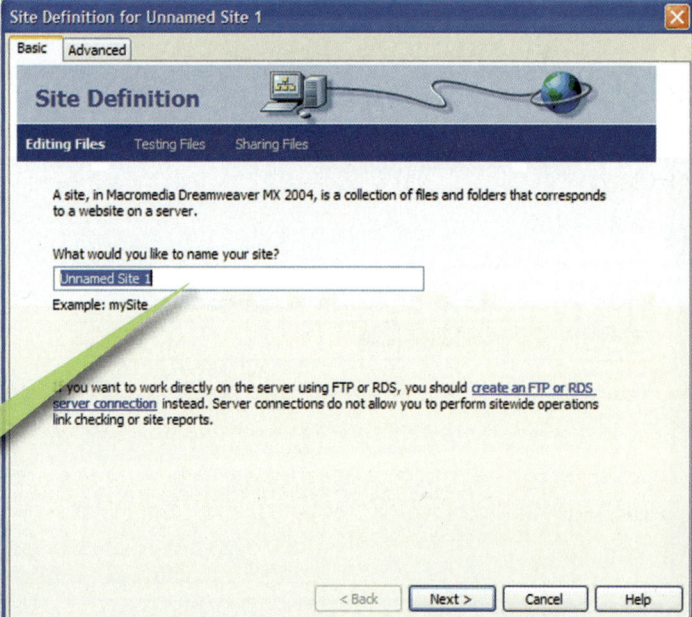

3 Type in a name for your site. Press

Next >

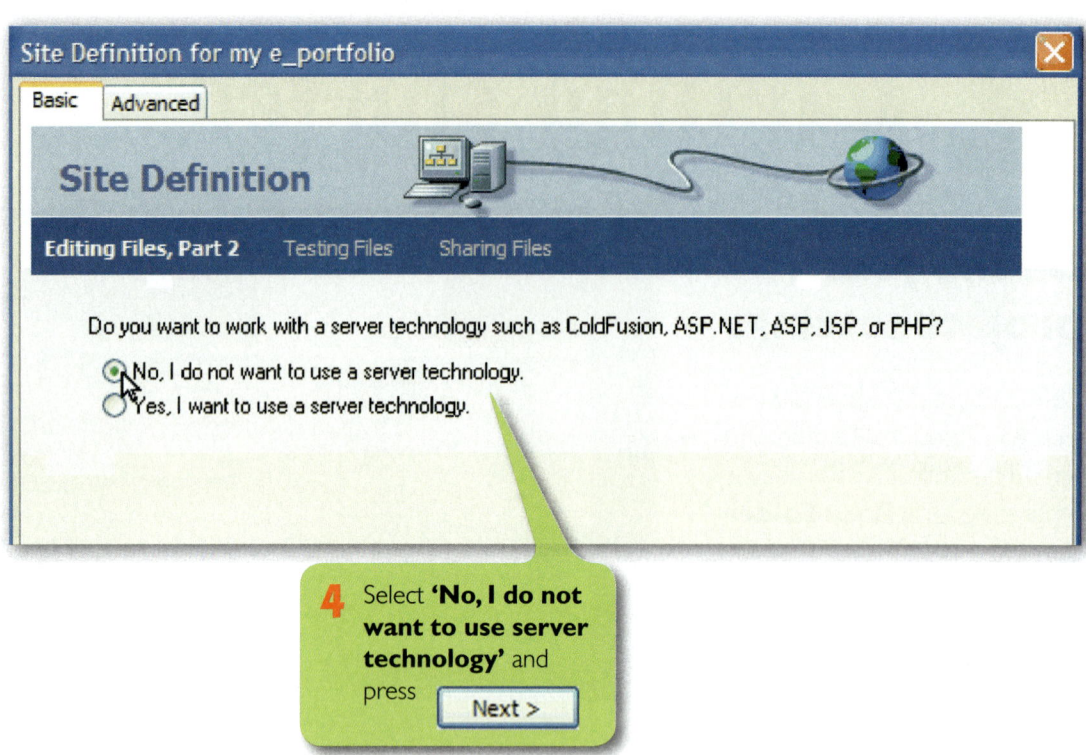

4 Select **'No, I do not want to use server technology'** and press [Next >]

5 Select **'Edit local copies on my machine'**. Select [Next >]

Click on the folder icon and choose the location for your root folder.

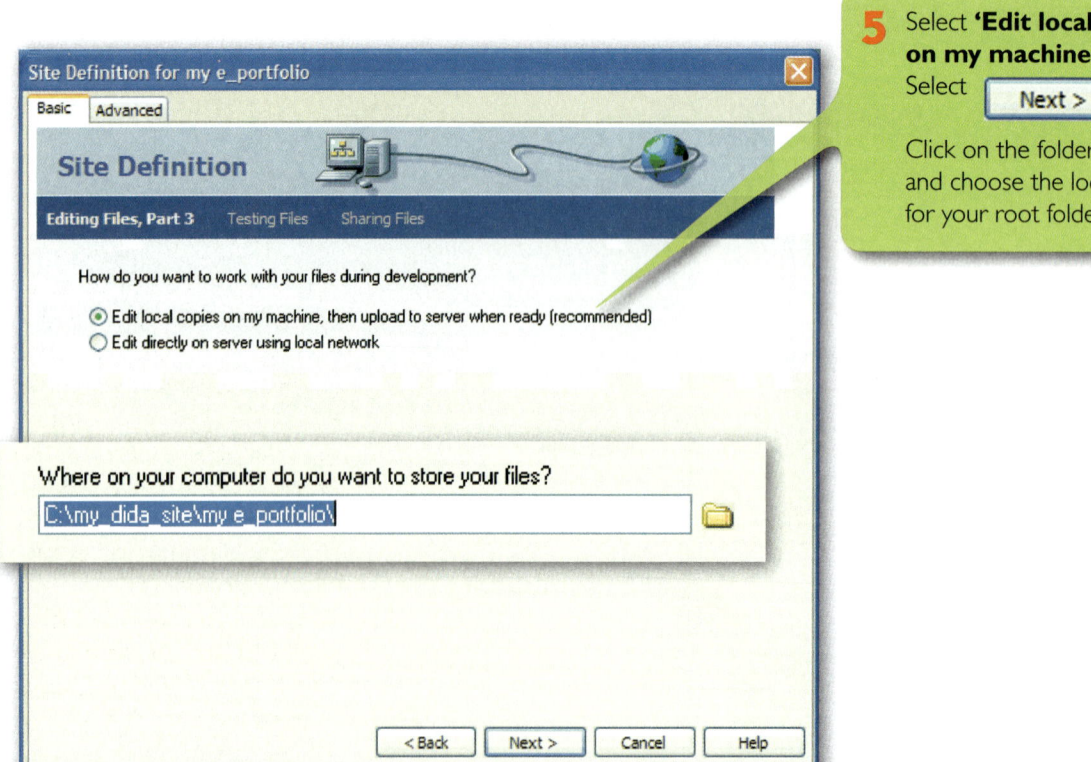

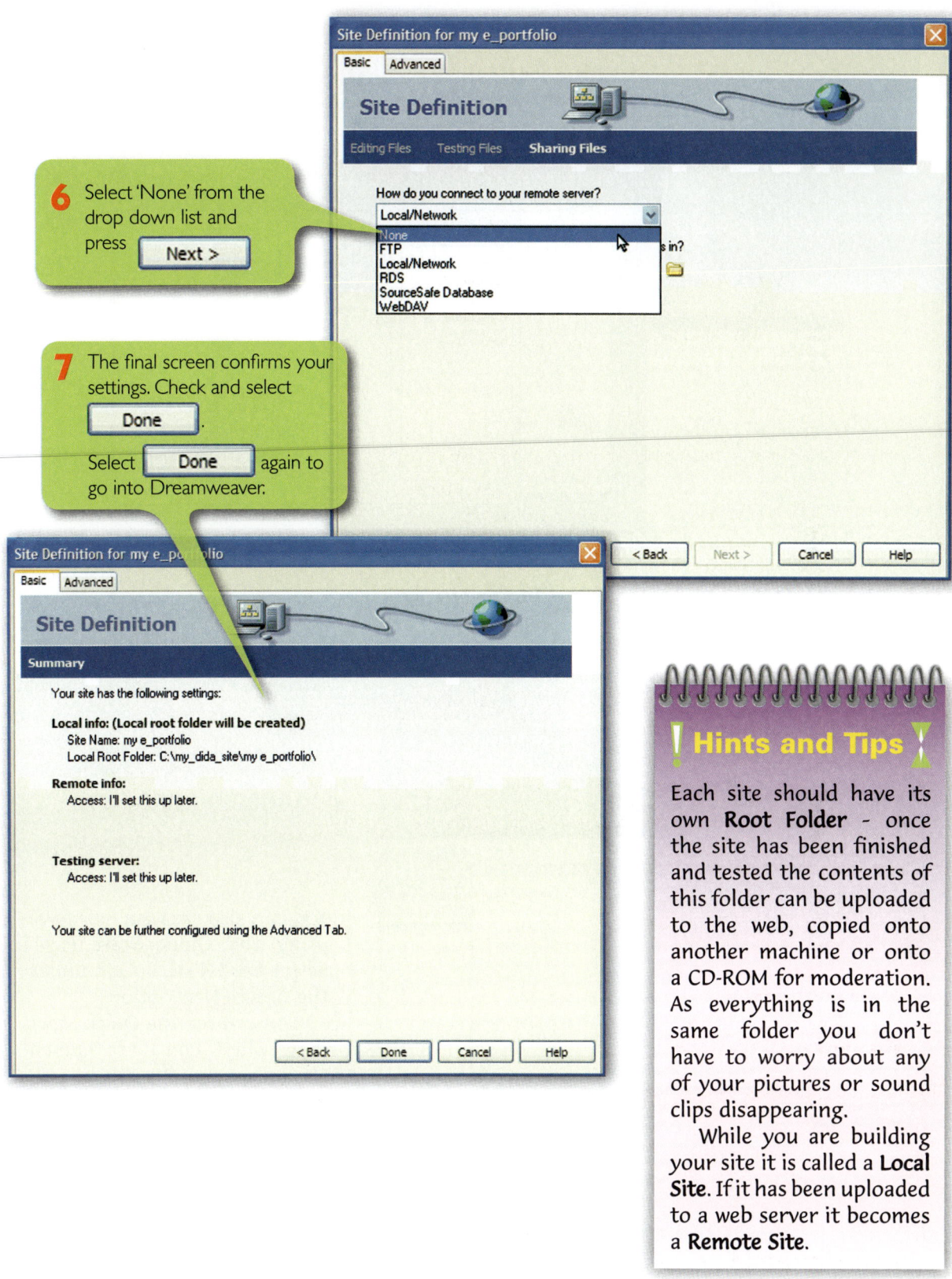

6 Select 'None' from the drop down list and press **Next >**

Site Definition for my e_portfolio

Basic | Advanced

Site Definition

Editing Files   Testing Files   **Sharing Files**

How do you connect to your remote server?

Local/Network

None
FTP
Local/Network
RDS
SourceSafe Database
WebDAV

7 The final screen confirms your settings. Check and select **Done**.

Select **Done** again to go into Dreamweaver.

< Back   Next >   Cancel   Help

Site Definition for my e_portfolio

Basic | Advanced

Site Definition

Summary

Your site has the following settings:

Local info: (Local root folder will be created)
Site Name: my e_portfolio
Local Root Folder: C:\my_dida_site\my e_portfolio\

Remote info:
Access: I'll set this up later.

Testing server:
Access: I'll set this up later.

Your site can be further configured using the Advanced Tab.

< Back   Done   Cancel   Help

! Hints and Tips !

Each site should have its own **Root Folder** - once the site has been finished and tested the contents of this folder can be uploaded to the web, copied onto another machine or onto a CD-ROM for moderation. As everything is in the same folder you don't have to worry about any of your pictures or sound clips disappearing.

While you are building your site it is called a **Local Site**. If it has been uploaded to a web server it becomes a **Remote Site**.

Create a new document

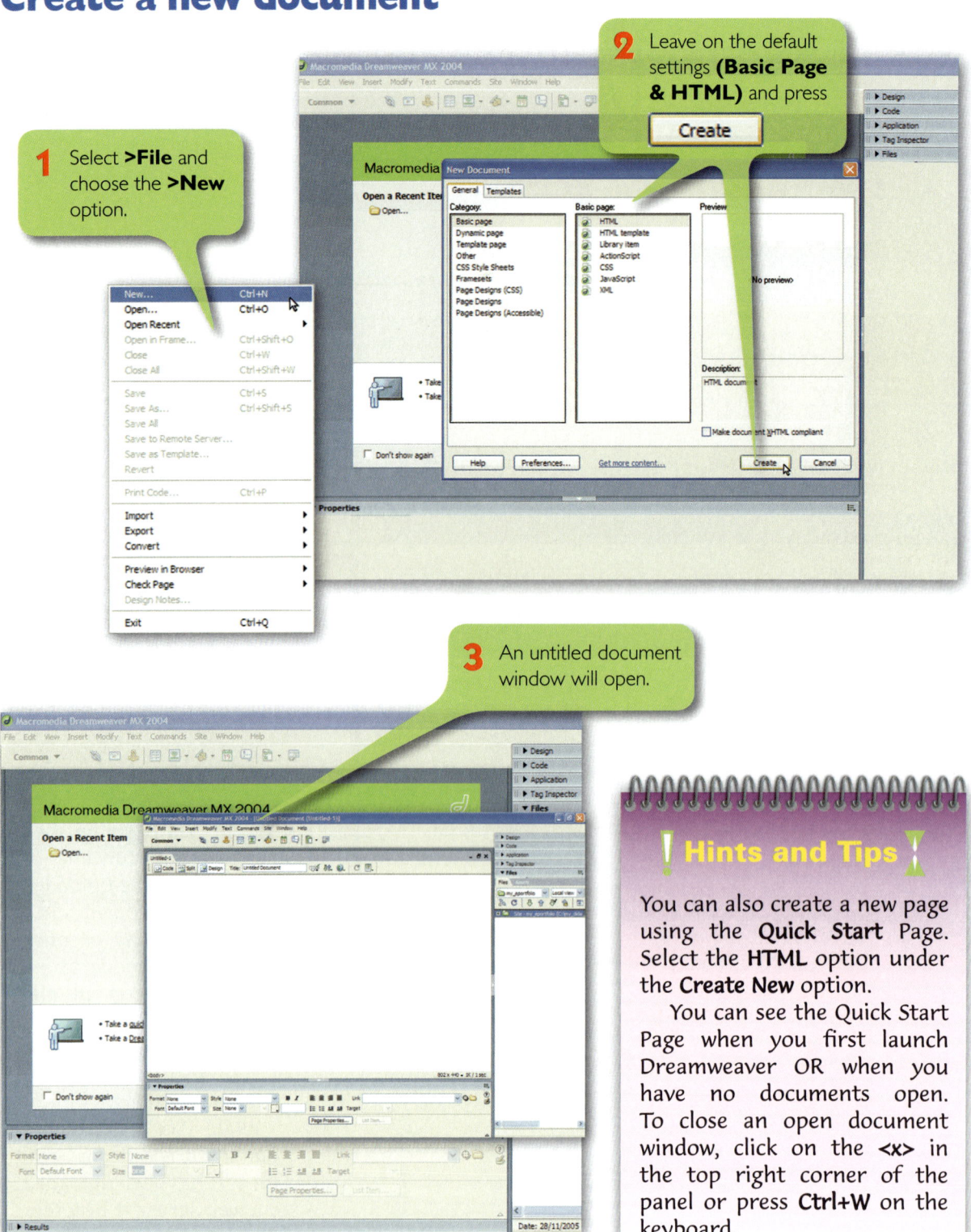

2 Leave on the default settings **(Basic Page & HTML)** and press

Create

1 Select **>File** and choose the **>New** option.

3 An untitled document window will open.

Hints and Tips

You can also create a new page using the **Quick Start** Page. Select the **HTML** option under the **Create New** option.

You can see the Quick Start Page when you first launch Dreamweaver OR when you have no documents open. To close an open document window, click on the **<x>** in the top right corner of the panel or press **Ctrl+W** on the keyboard.

The key elements of your workspace

The key elements of the Dreamweaver MX 2004 workspace are shown below.

7 **Panels Groups** are sets of related panels grouped together depending on function. To select an individual panel click the tab, to expand or collapse the panel, click the arrow to the left of each heading.

1 The **Insert Bar** contains buttons for inserting different types of 'objects' into a document, such as graphics and media into the pages of your site. It acts as your 'tool box'.

6 The **Files Panel** lets you manage the files and folders you need for your site and to access all of the files on your computer.

2 The **Document Toolbar** contains buttons and pop-up menus that let you change your view of the document window.

3 The **Document Window** acts as your 'canvas' and allows you to visually build your web pages. Use the tab(s) along the top to select an open document.

5 **The Status Bar** contains the **Tag Selector** on the left and the **Page Weight** field on the right. The Page Weight shows the file size of the page and the estimated download time.

4 The **Properties panel** allows you to change the properties of the selected object or text. Change the font, size and colour of that text. Select an image to change the width and height of the image.

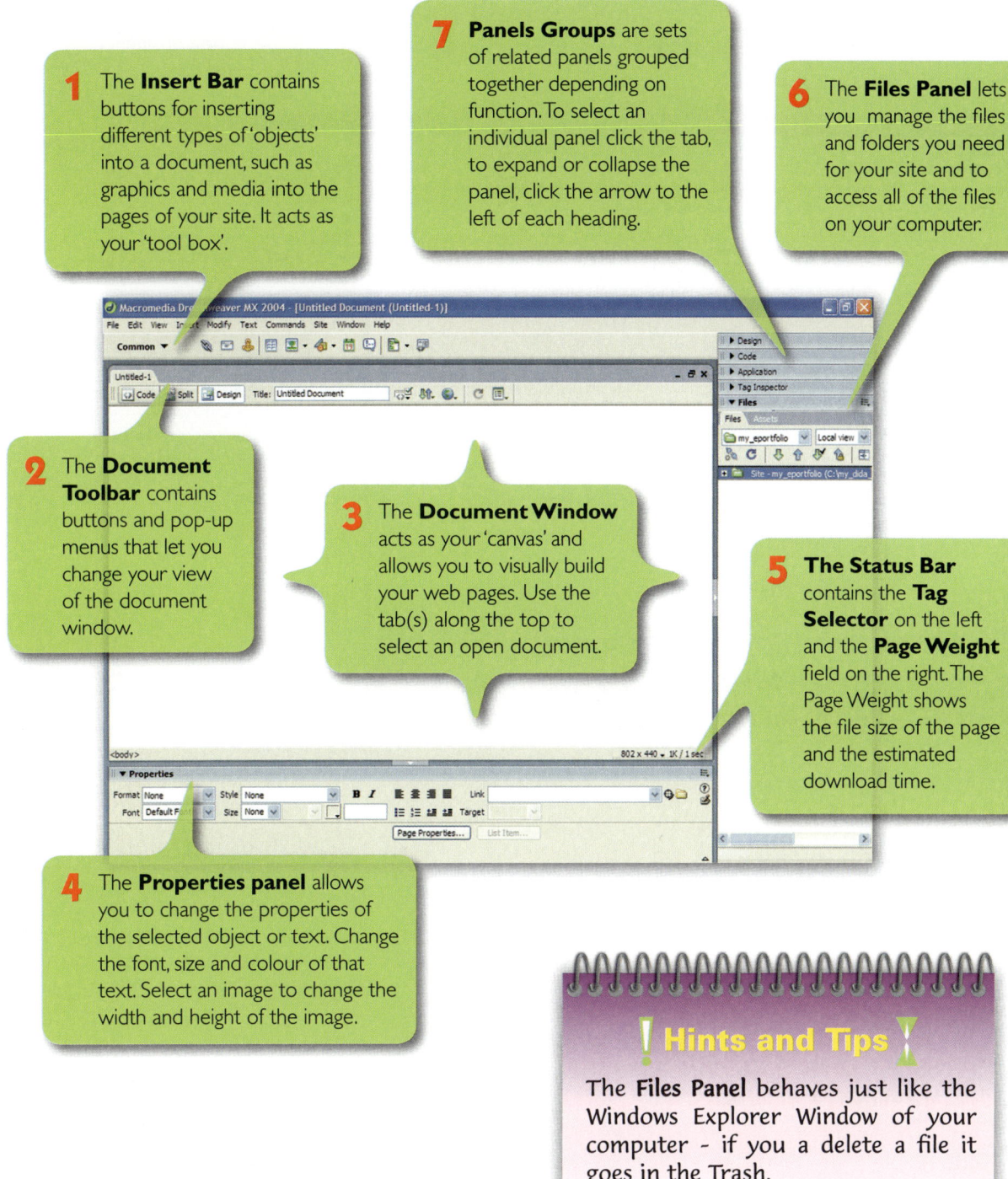

Hints and Tips

The **Files Panel** behaves just like the Windows Explorer Window of your computer - if you a delete a file it goes in the Trash.

Change the layout of the panels

The layout of the screen can be changed to suit you. Most windows, panels and panel groups can be expanded, collapsed and closed.

Expand/Collapse a Panel

1 Click on the arrow button or title for each panel.

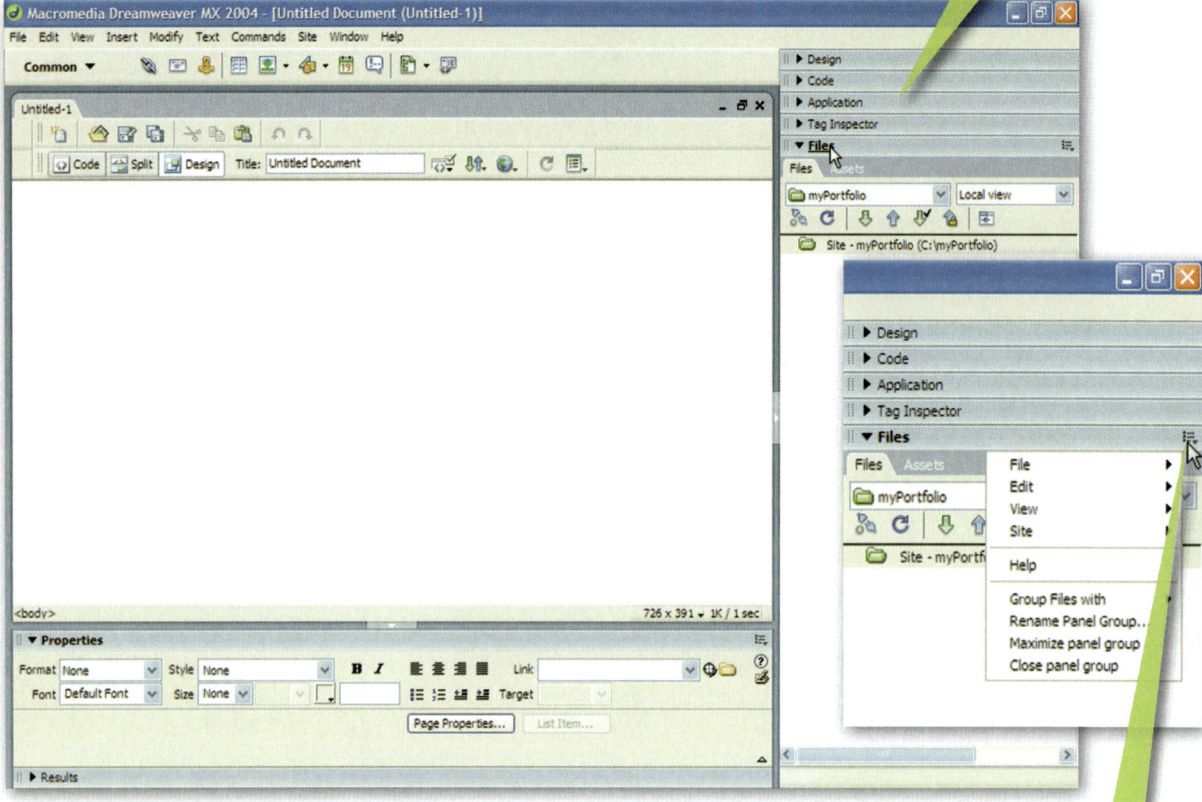

2 When expanded, an options menu icon is shown in the right hand corner – click to view a list of features specific to that panel.

! Hints and Tips !

If you 'lose' a panel, use the **>Window** option on the Main Task Bar to re-open the required window.

Change the views

The three buttons on the left of your document toolbar allow you to toggle between the main working views. These enable you to check and review your work.

2 The **SPLIT View** button splits the document window to show the code and the visual content.

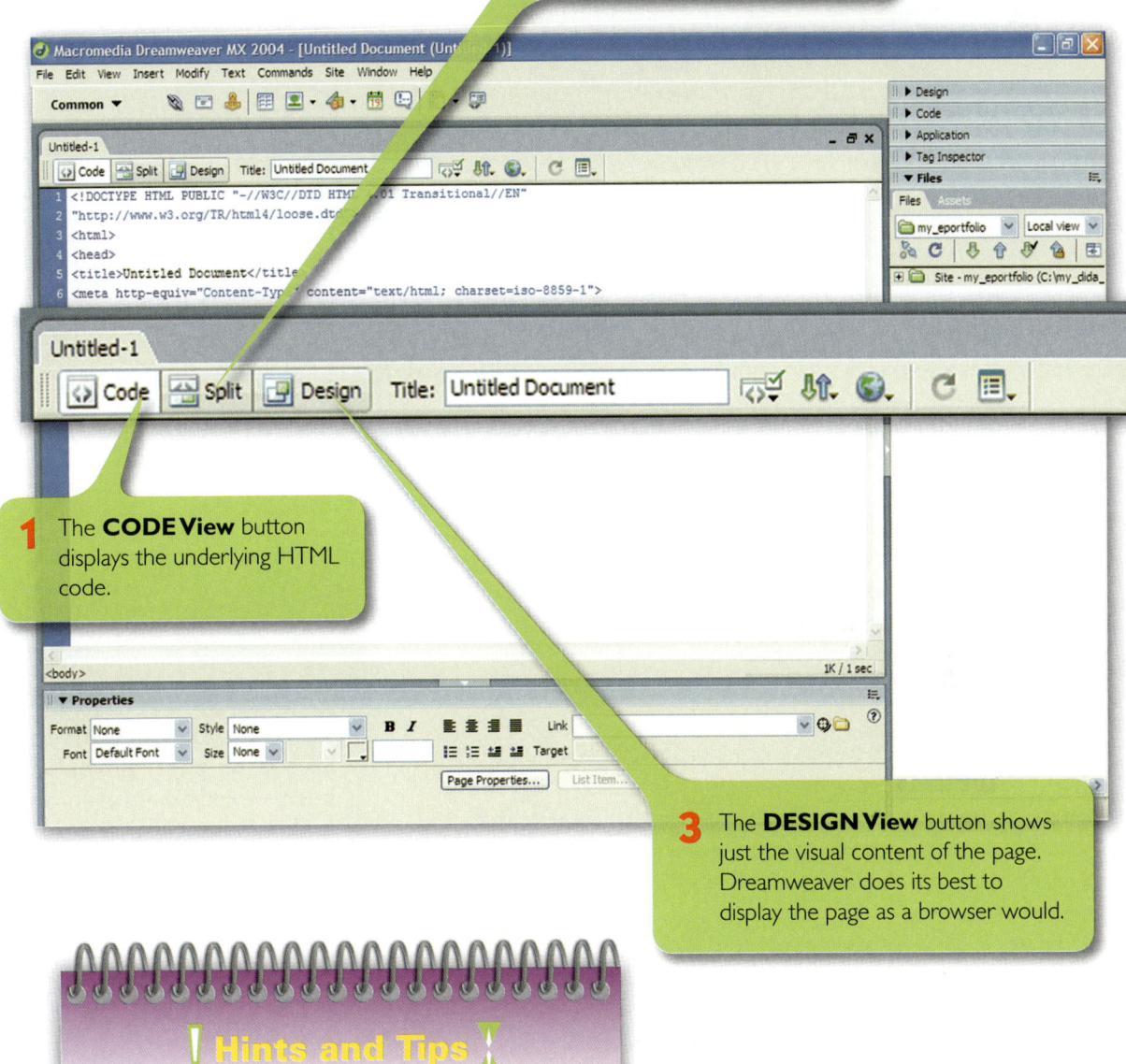

1 The **CODE View** button displays the underlying HTML code.

3 The **DESIGN View** button shows just the visual content of the page. Dreamweaver does its best to display the page as a browser would.

! Hints and Tips !

When you are creating your E-portfolio you will be using the Design view.

Close a document

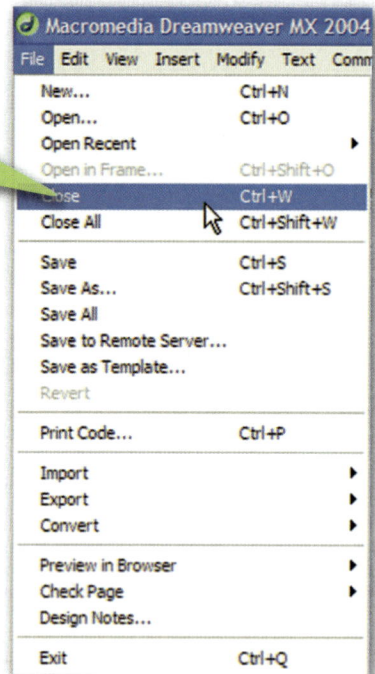

1 To close a document, click on the ⊠ in the top right hand corner of the document window, OR select **>File >Close** OR press **Ctrl+W** on the keyboard.

2 If a change has been made, a prompt will appear asking if you wish to save **<Yes>** or **<No>**.

Over to you

Open the Food Matters! Project and navigate to the E-portfolio page. Read through the checklist to make sure that you know what evidence is needed.

You need to create a directory structure to store your evidence (Student Book page 16). This lets you plan for your work on the project. Then you need to plan your E-portfolio to showcase this work and you can use your directory structure to help you.

Your E-portfolio will be a set of web pages and the evidence from your project so you need to set up a logical structure so that your audience can move about easily. Remember that the portfolio will contain evidence of:

● How you got your information
● Your publications themselves and commentaries on how you developed them
● How you managed the project
● A review of the whole project.

Use the E-portfolio checklist to create a structure diagram for your Food Matters! E-portfolio. Look at pages 139 and 140 of the Student Book to help you.

! Hints and Tips !

Normally you will want to save your page. If you've been experimenting or making changes you don't want to keep, closing the window without saving allows you to return to a previously saved version.

3 Build a basic web page

This section outlines the basic techniques required to create a simple web page containing text and images. On completion, you will have created an example of an E-Portfolio home page.

Create and save a page

1 To create a new page, select **>File** and choose the **>New** option. Leave on the default settings **(Basic Page & HTML)** and press Create .

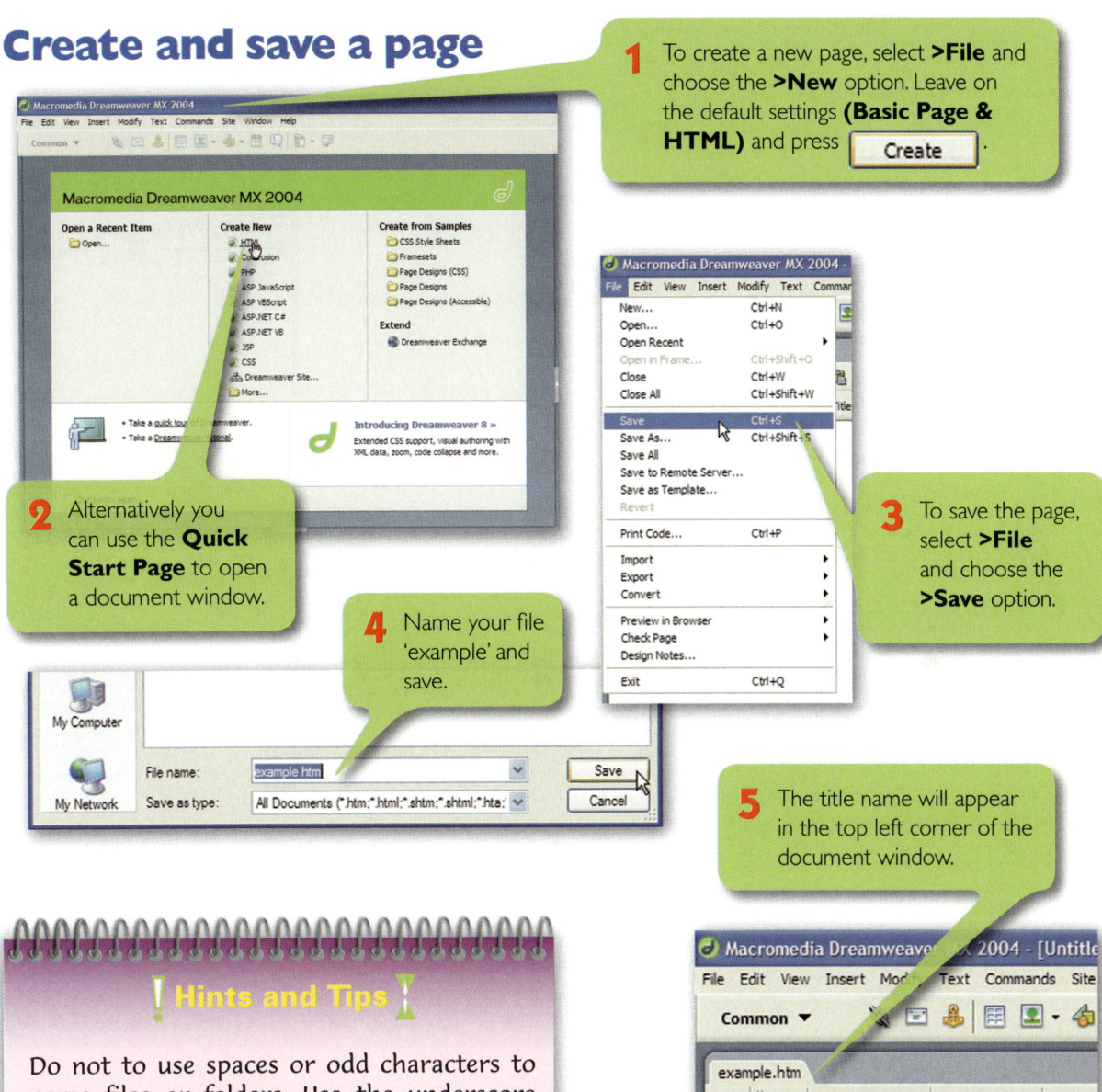

2 Alternatively you can use the **Quick Start Page** to open a document window.

3 To save the page, select **>File** and choose the **>Save** option.

4 Name your file 'example' and save.

5 The title name will appear in the top left corner of the document window.

! Hints and Tips !

Do not to use spaces or odd characters to name files or folders. Use the underscore character ('_') instead.

Add and format text using the style options

1 Open your **'example'** file.

2 Click the cursor inside the document window and type 'Welcome to My E-Portfolio'.

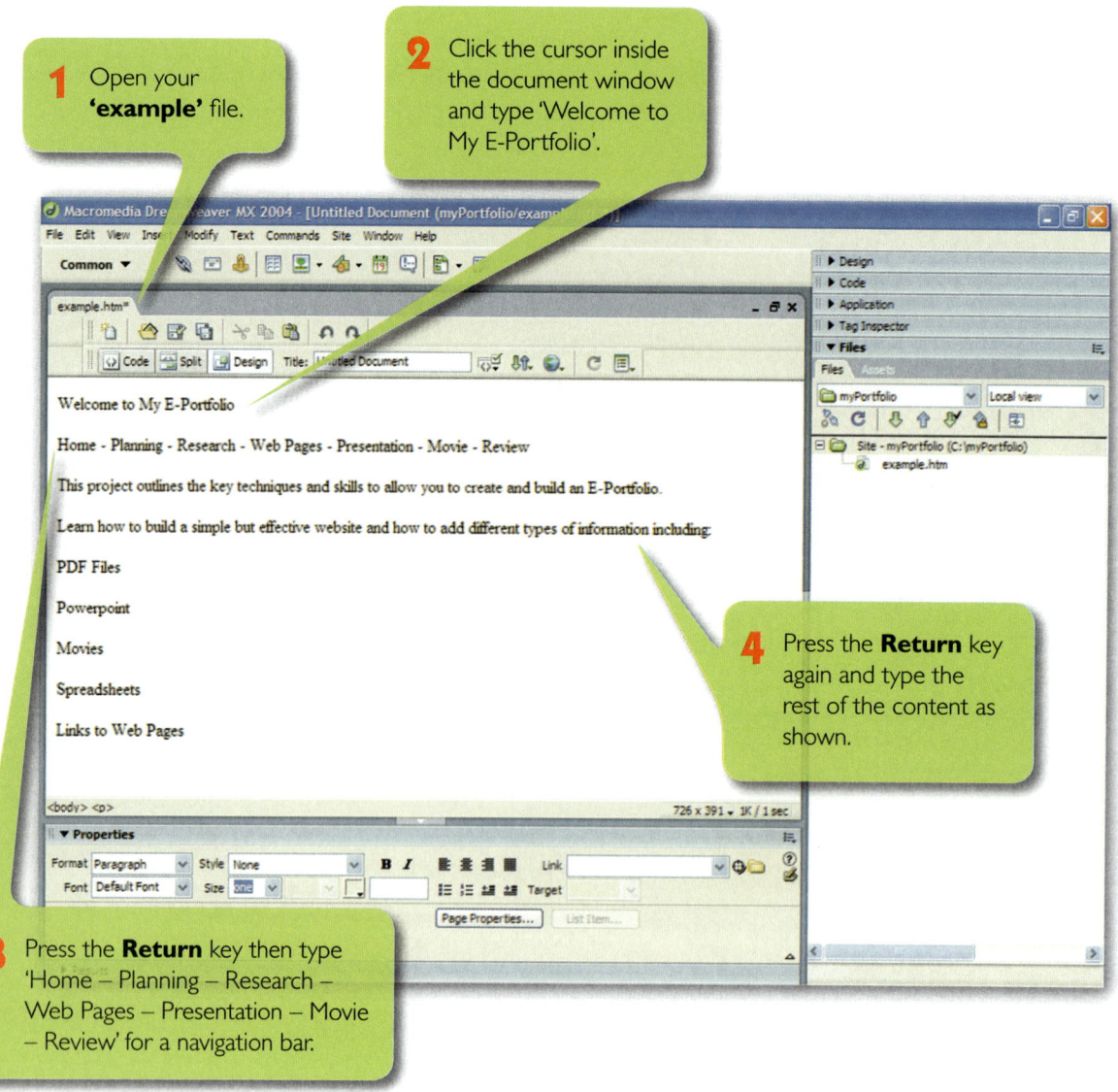

4 Press the **Return** key again and type the rest of the content as shown.

3 Press the **Return** key then type 'Home – Planning – Research – Web Pages – Presentation – Movie – Review' for a navigation bar.

5 Highlight the first line of text.

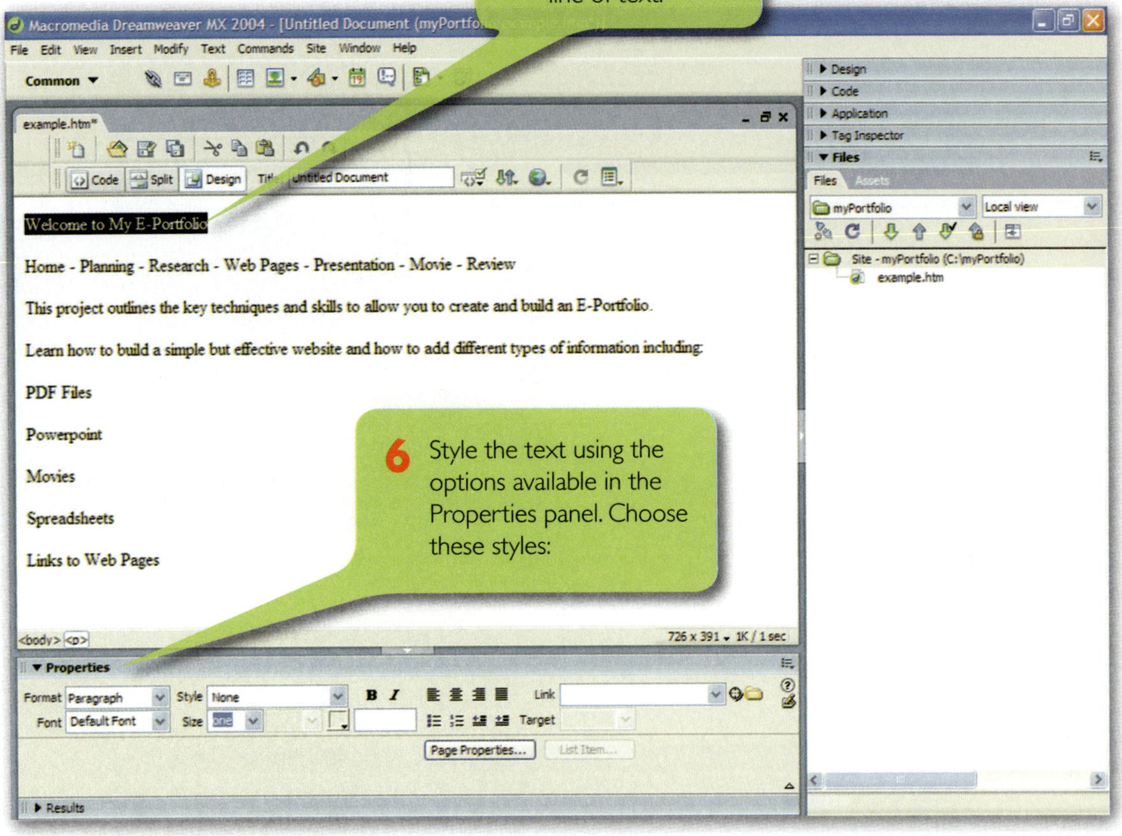

Macromedia Dreamweaver MX 2004 - [Untitled Document (myPortfolio...

File Edit View Insert Modify Text Commands Site Window Help

Common ▼

example.htm*

Code | Split | Design | Title: Untitled Document

Welcome to My E-Portfolio

Home - Planning - Research - Web Pages - Presentation - Movie - Review

This project outlines the key techniques and skills to allow you to create and build an E-Portfolio.

Learn how to build a simple but effective website and how to add different types of information including:

PDF Files

Powerpoint

Movies

Spreadsheets

Links to Web Pages

6 Style the text using the options available in the Properties panel. Choose these styles:

<body> <p>   726 x 391 ▾ 1K / 1 sec

▼ Properties

Format Paragraph ▾ Style None ▾ **B** *I* Link

Font Default Font ▾ Size None ▾ Target

Page Properties... List Item...

▶ Results

▶ Design
▶ Code
▶ Application
▶ Tag Inspector
▼ Files

Files Assets

myPortfolio ▾ Local view ▾

Site - myPortfolio (C:\myPortfolio)
    example.htm

---

7 Font – set to 'Arial, Helvetica, San Serif'

Default Font
Arial, Helvetica, sans-serif
Times New Roman, Times, serif
Courier New, Courier, mono
Georgia, Times New Roman, Times, serif
Verdana, Arial, Helvetica, sans-serif
Geneva, Arial, Helvetica, sans-serif
GillSans
Edit Font List...

8 Size – set to 'xx-large'.

None
9
10
12
14
16
18
24
36
xx-small
x-small
small
medium
large
x-large
xx-large
smaller
larger

10 Text Style - set to 'BOLD'

B *I*
#FF6600
Bold

9 Colour – use '#FF6600' (orange)

11 Text Position – 'Align Centre'

Link
Target 1 sec
Align Center

Style style.3 ▾ **B** *I* Link
Font ca, sans-serif ▾ Size xx-la ▾ #FF6600 Target

#FF6600

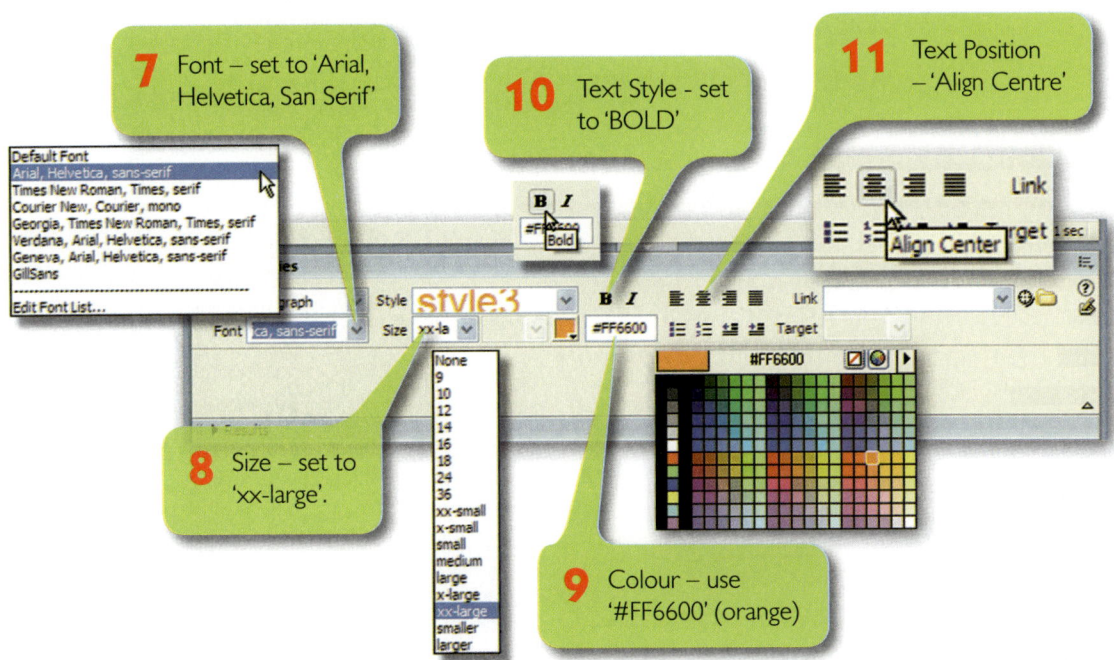

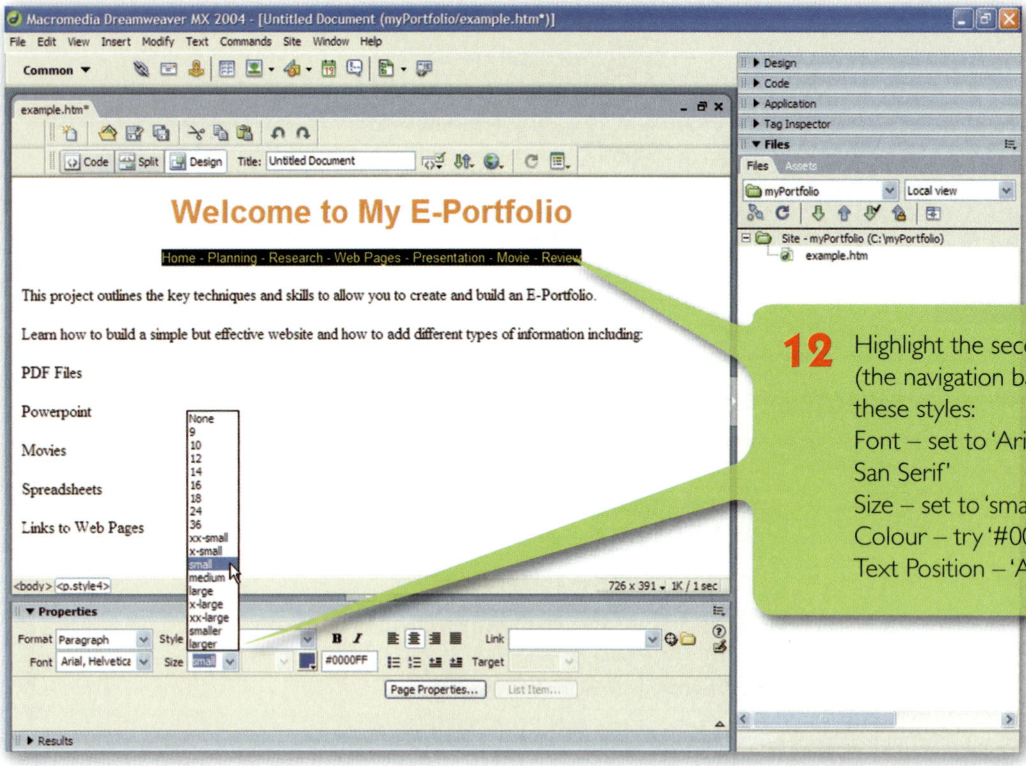

12 Highlight the second line of text (the navigation bar) and apply these styles:
Font – set to 'Arial, Helvetica, San Serif'
Size – set to 'small'
Colour – try '#0000FF' (blue)
Text Position – 'Align Centre'

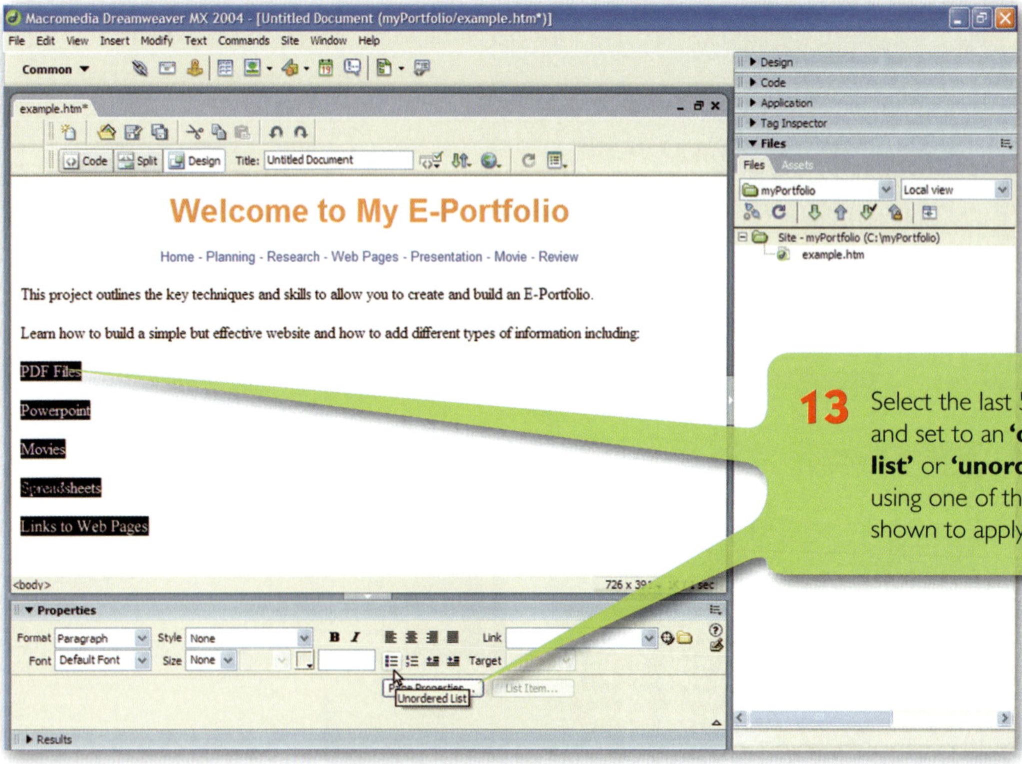

13 Select the last 5 lines of text and set to an **'ordered list'** or **'unordered list'** using one of the two options shown to apply bullet points.

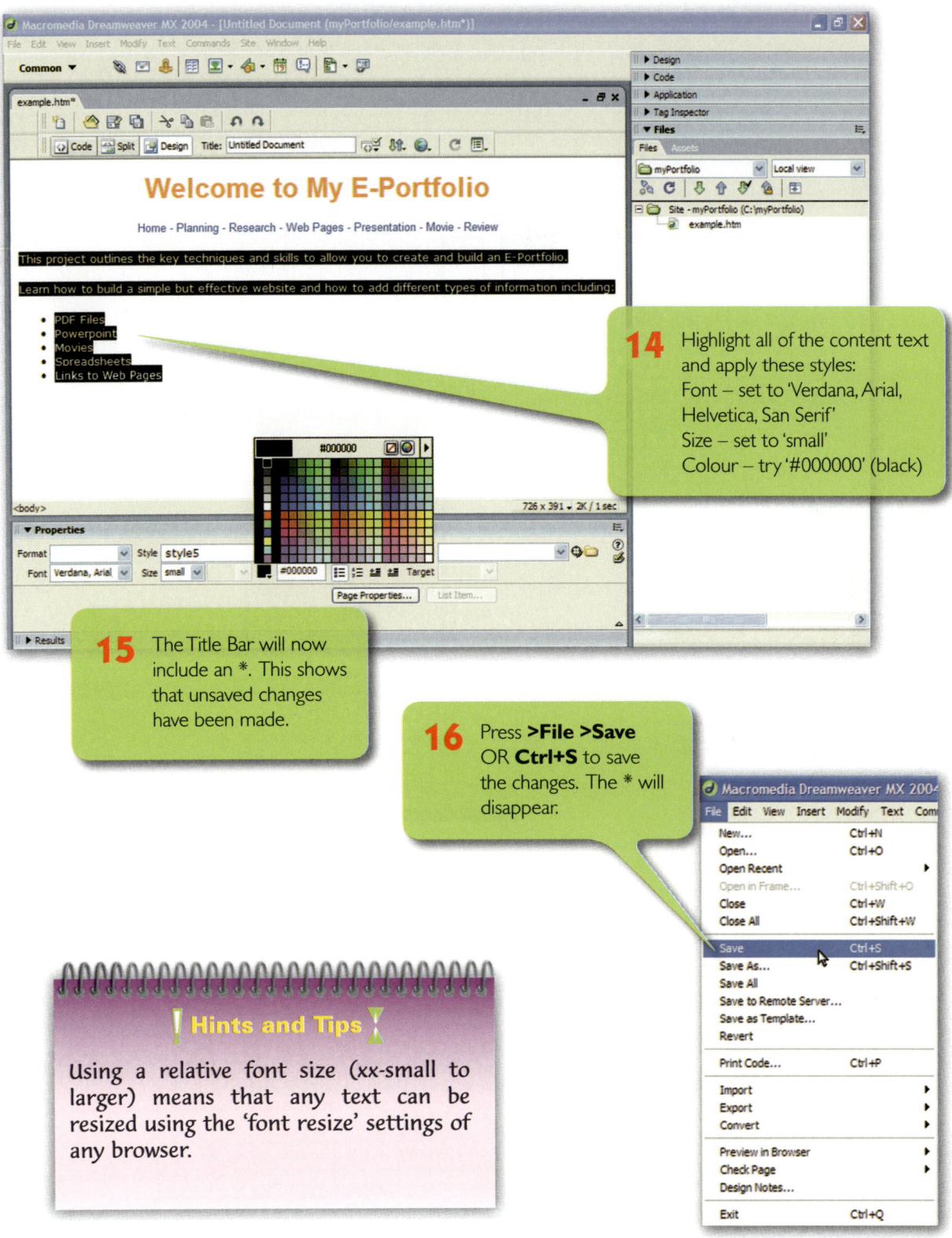

14 Highlight all of the content text and apply these styles:
Font – set to 'Verdana, Arial, Helvetica, San Serif'
Size – set to 'small'
Colour – try '#000000' (black)

15 The Title Bar will now include an *. This shows that unsaved changes have been made.

16 Press **>File >Save** OR **Ctrl+S** to save the changes. The * will disappear.

! Hints and Tips !

Using a relative font size (xx-small to larger) means that any text can be resized using the 'font resize' settings of any browser.

Format text using the format options

You can also format the text using the Format options. These are similar to applying styles in Microsoft Word where you can define and apply styles for a Heading, a Title, Paragraph text, etc. If you then change the colour or size of a Heading, it will be applied to all the pages rather than just to a single entry.

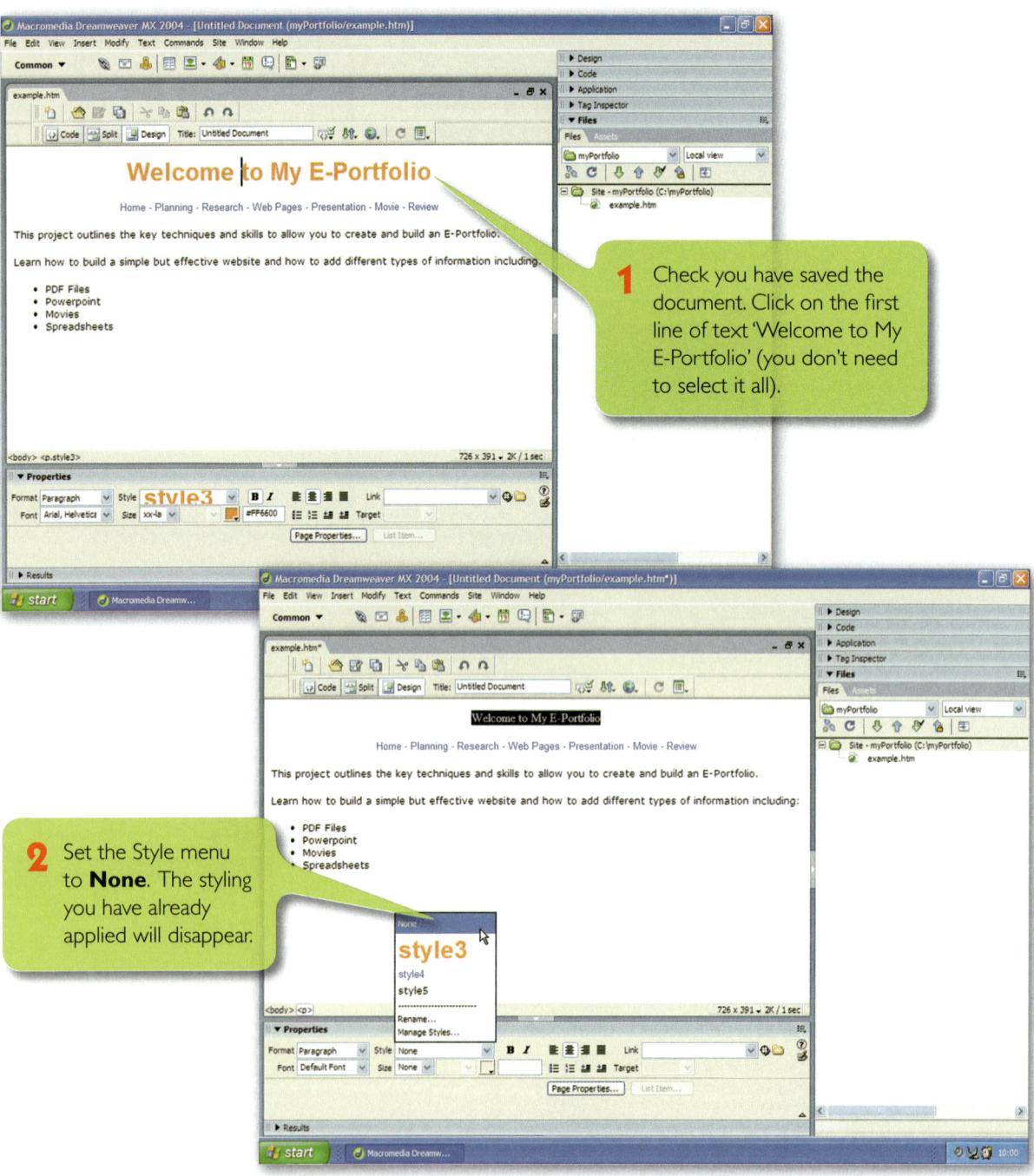

1 Check you have saved the document. Click on the first line of text 'Welcome to My E-Portfolio' (you don't need to select it all).

2 Set the Style menu to **None**. The styling you have already applied will disappear.

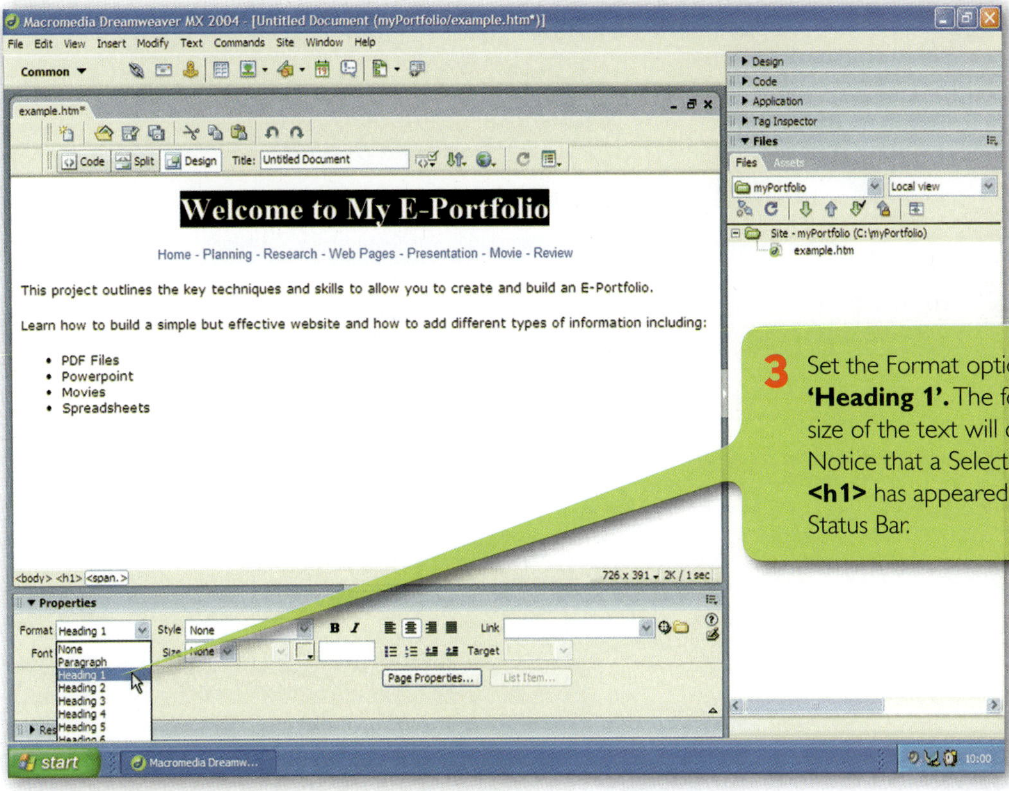

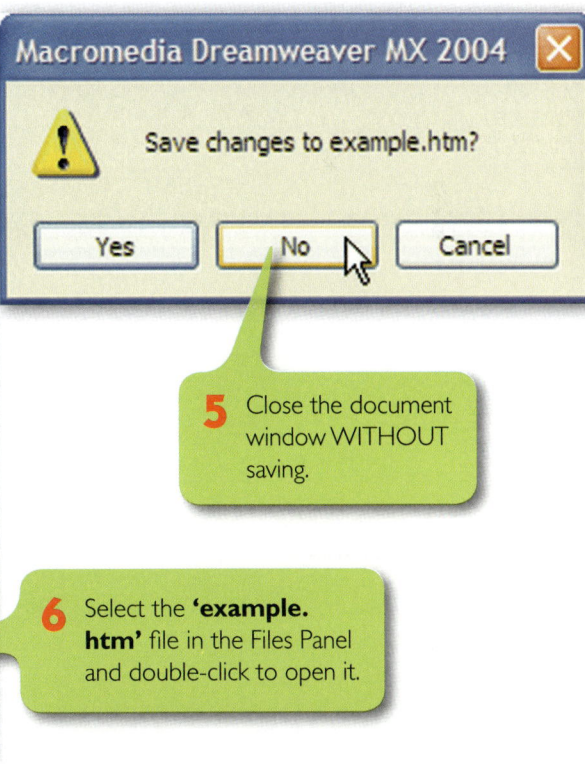

3 Set the Format option to **'Heading 1'.** The font and size of the text will change. Notice that a Selector Tag **<h1>** has appeared on the Status Bar.

4 Click on the second line of text and set the Style menu to **None.**
Set the Format option to **'Heading 5'** – the text will change again and a Selector Tag **<h5>** appears on the Status Bar.

5 Close the document window WITHOUT saving.

6 Select the **'example. htm'** file in the Files Panel and double-click to open it.

Insert a rule

1 Click the mouse at the end of the second line of text (the navigation bar) – a flashing cursor will appear. Press the **Return** key to create a line break. Change the Insert Panel from **Common** to **HTML**.

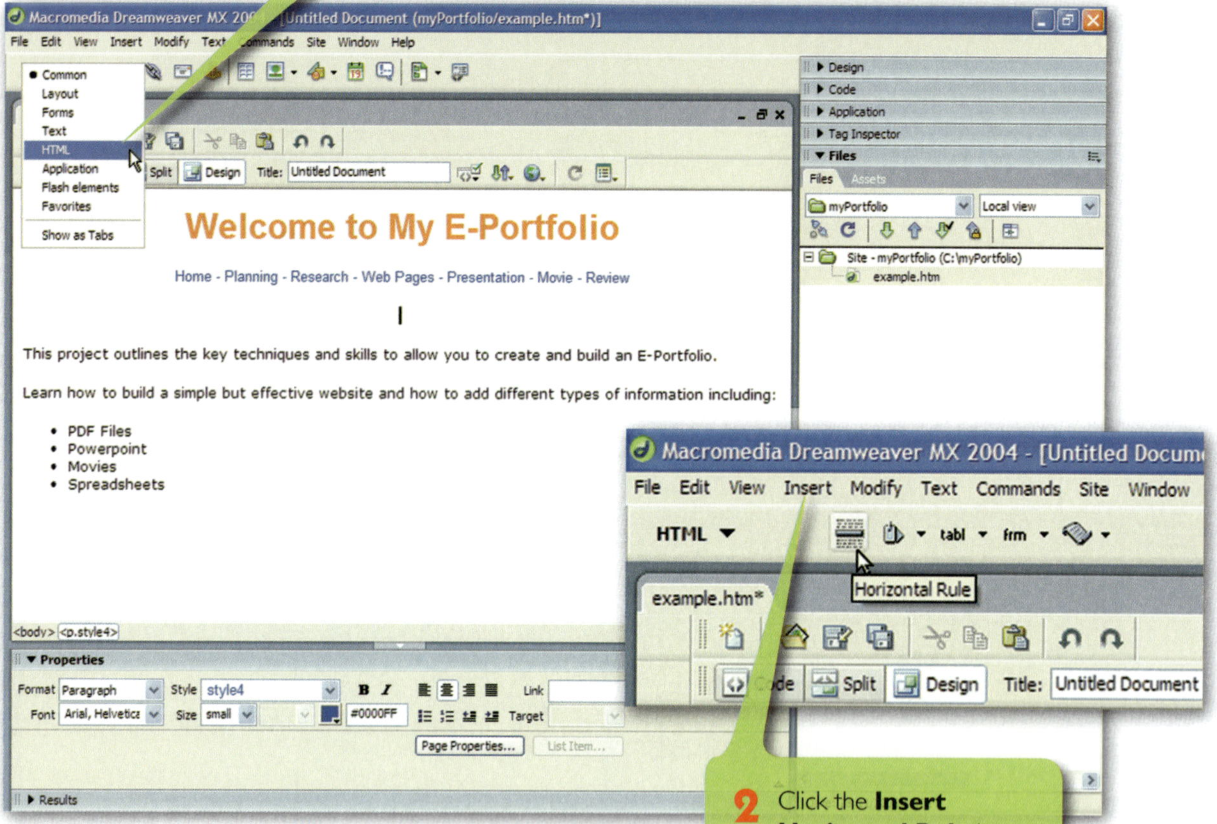

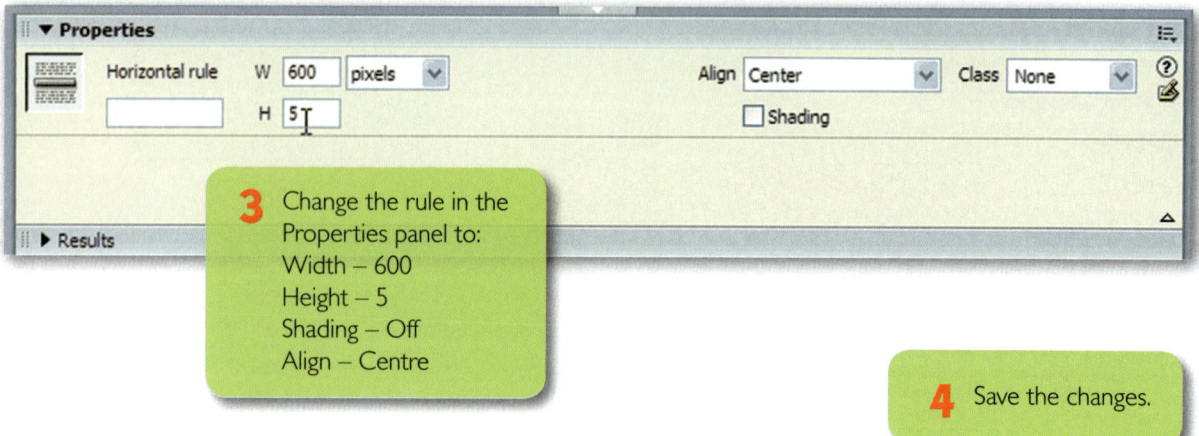

2 Click the **Insert Horizontal Rule** icon.

3 Change the rule in the Properties panel to:
Width – 600
Height – 5
Shading – Off
Align – Centre

4 Save the changes.

Insert a GIF or JPEG graphic

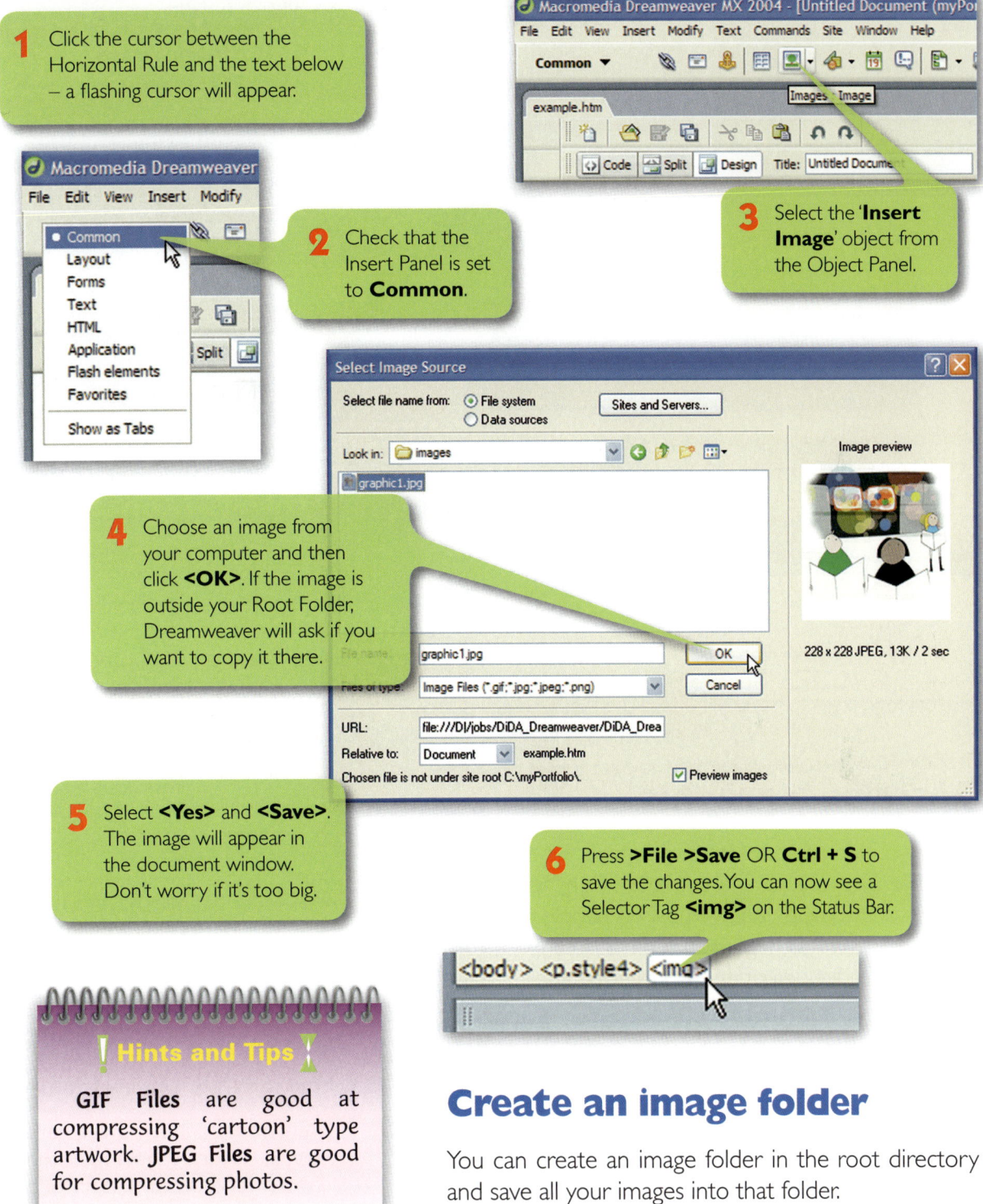

1 Click the cursor between the Horizontal Rule and the text below – a flashing cursor will appear.

2 Check that the Insert Panel is set to **Common**.

3 Select the '**Insert Image**' object from the Object Panel.

4 Choose an image from your computer and then click **<OK>**. If the image is outside your Root Folder, Dreamweaver will ask if you want to copy it there.

5 Select **<Yes>** and **<Save>**. The image will appear in the document window. Don't worry if it's too big.

6 Press **>File >Save** OR **Ctrl + S** to save the changes. You can now see a Selector Tag **<img>** on the Status Bar.

Hints and Tips

GIF Files are good at compressing 'cartoon' type artwork. **JPEG Files** are good for compressing photos.

Create an image folder

You can create an image folder in the root directory and save all your images into that folder.
See the section 'Maintain your E-Portfolio' on page 64.

Resize a graphic

1 Select the graphic with a single click – a black bounding box with three resizing handles will appear.

2 Go to the Properties panel and check the image is set to **'Align Centre'**.

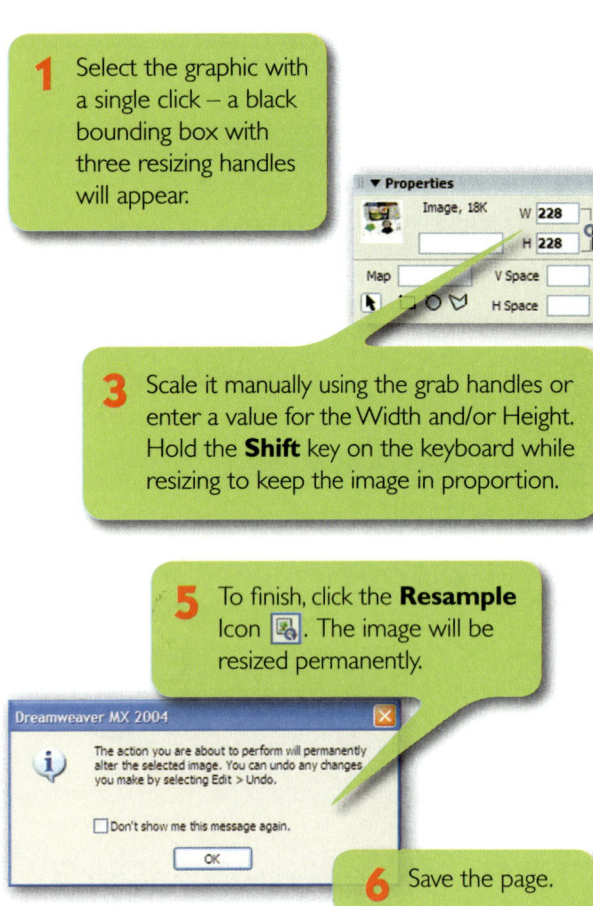

3 Scale it manually using the grab handles or enter a value for the Width and/or Height. Hold the **Shift** key on the keyboard while resizing to keep the image in proportion.

4 To reset the image to its original size, click on the blue circular **Reset** icon.

5 To finish, click the **Resample** Icon 🖼. The image will be resized permanently.

Dreamweaver MX 2004

ⓘ The action you are about to perform will permanently alter the selected image. You can undo any changes you make by selecting Edit > Undo.

☐ Don't show me this message again.

[OK]

6 Save the page.

Hints and Tips

You can also use the Crop, Brightness/Contrast and Sharpen tools. If you make changes using the Crop Tool, press the Return key to apply the changes.

Describe a graphic

When you are creating your E-portfolio you must make sure that everyone can access your work. 'Text readers' can be used to help visually impaired people access text. You can use an 'alt tag' to include a description of an image to give an idea of the message the image is giving.

1 Select the graphic with a single click. Go to the Properties panel and describe the graphic in the **'Alt'** field. Press the **Return** key.

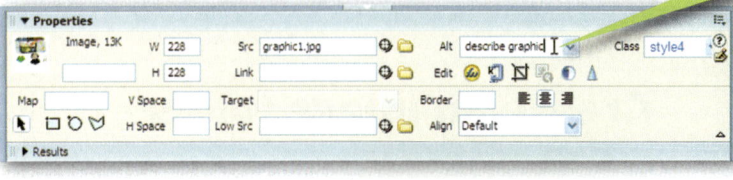

2 Save the page.

Hints and Tips

Remember that there are marks for making the contents of your E-portfolio accessible.

Preview a page in a browser

It's a good idea to preview your page in your web browser every now and then to see how your audience will view your work. You need to know how the page will look and behave for your teacher and the moderator.

1 Select **>File >Preview in Browser** – select the browser option(s) you want and the page will open in the browser window.

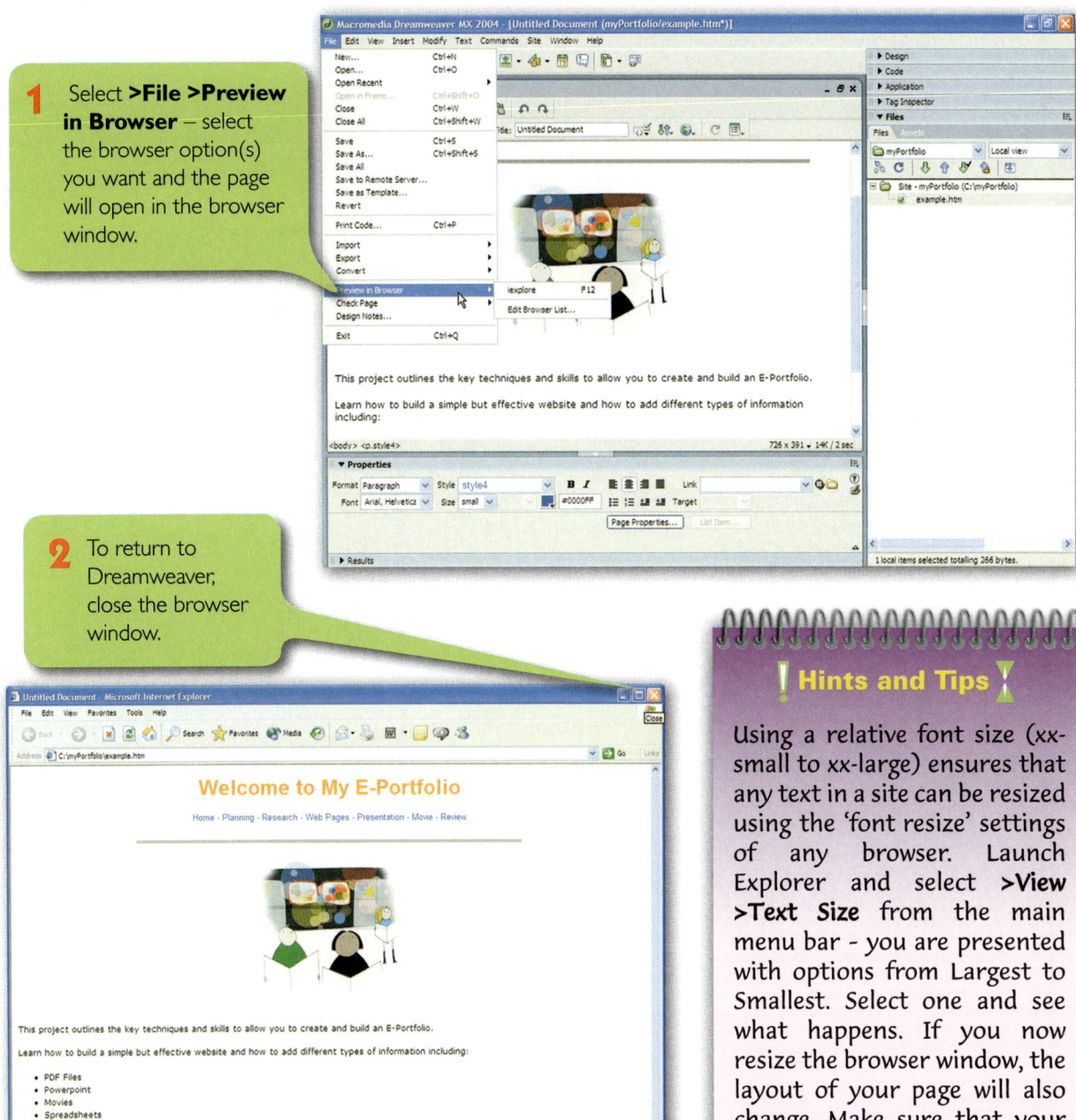

2 To return to Dreamweaver, close the browser window.

Hints and Tips

Using a relative font size (xx-small to xx-large) ensures that any text in a site can be resized using the 'font resize' settings of any browser. Launch Explorer and select **>View >Text Size** from the main menu bar - you are presented with options from Largest to Smallest. Select one and see what happens. If you now resize the browser window, the layout of your page will also change. Make sure that your screen is set to a resolution of 1024 x 768 pixels, which you need to use for DiDA.

Insert a table

You can use tables to help layout the pages of your E-portfolio. Each row or cell in the table can hold information such as text and images or even other tables.

1 Click the cursor at the end of the last bullet point, and press the **Return** key twice to create a new empty line.

2 Check the Insert Panel is set to **Common**.

3 Select the **Table** icon in the Insert Panel – the Table property panel will then appear.

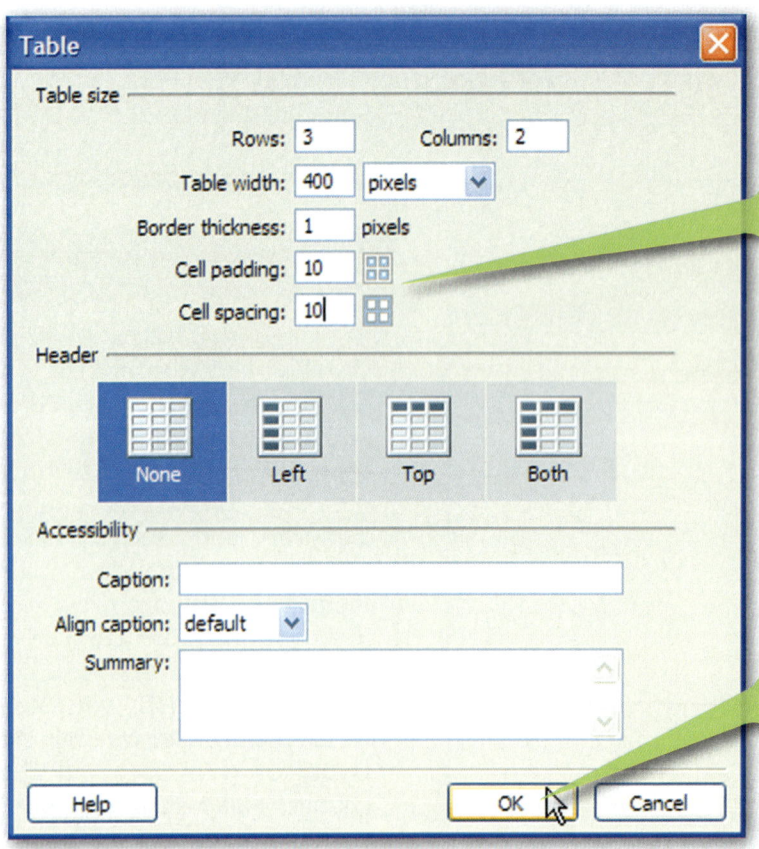

4 Set the Table properties panel to:
Rows – 3
Columns – 2
Width 400 Pixels
Border – 1
Cell Padding – 10
Cell Spacing – 10

5 Select **<OK>** and save the changes.

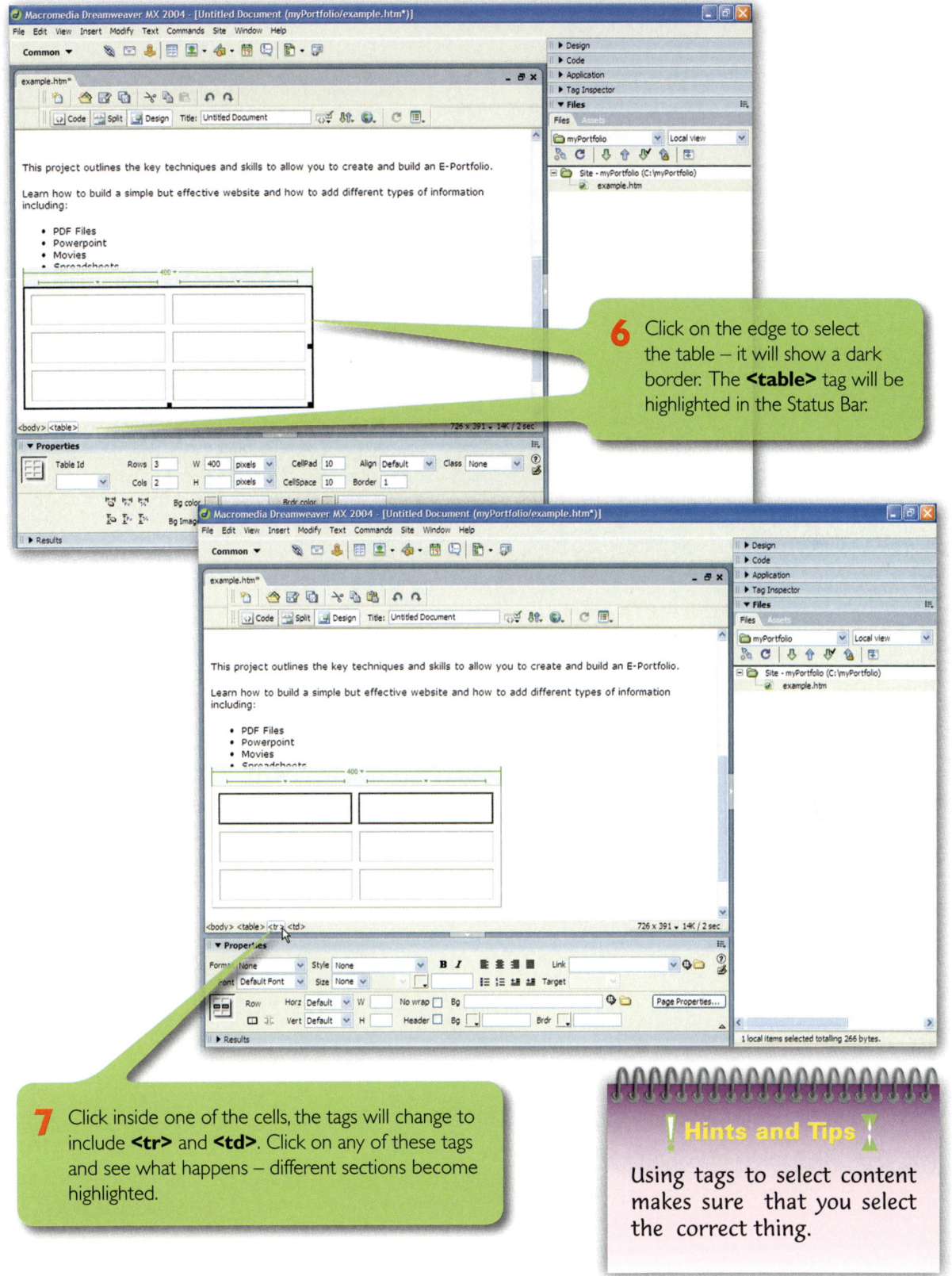

6 Click on the edge to select the table – it will show a dark border. The **<table>** tag will be highlighted in the Status Bar.

7 Click inside one of the cells, the tags will change to include **<tr>** and **<td>**. Click on any of these tags and see what happens – different sections become highlighted.

Merge selected cells or rows

The cells and rows within a table can be merged. This allows you to modify the table to best suit your page layout.

1 Select the two top cells.

2 Select the **'Merges selected cells using spans'** icon in the Properties panel. The two cells will merge.

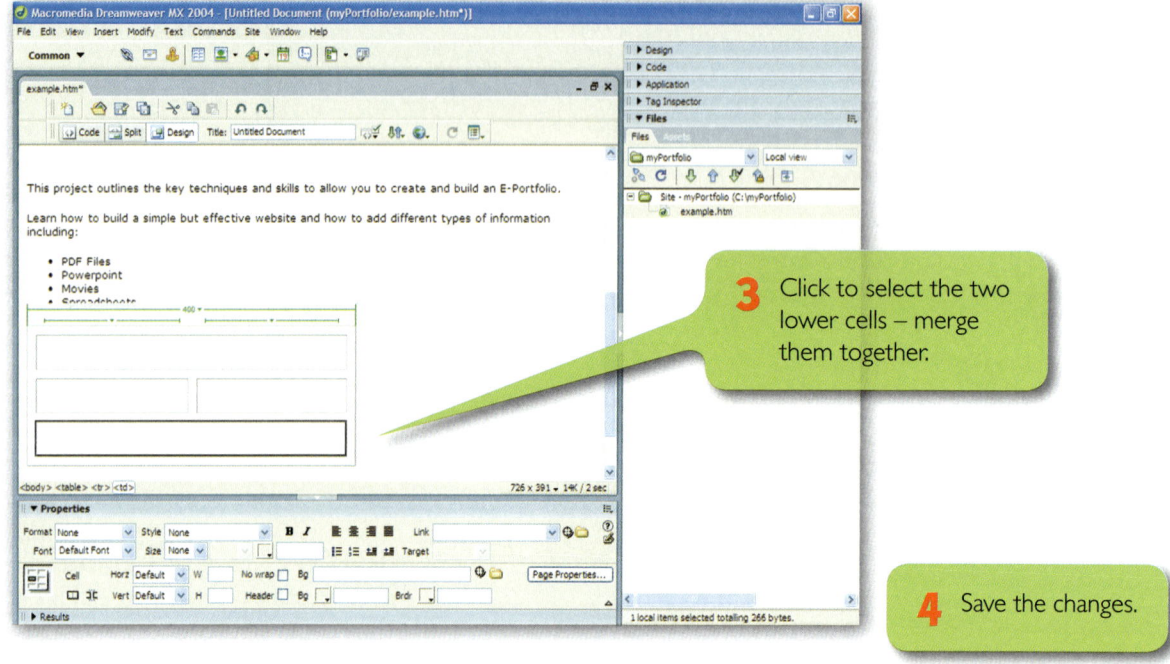

3 Click to select the two lower cells – merge them together.

4 Save the changes.

Colour a cell

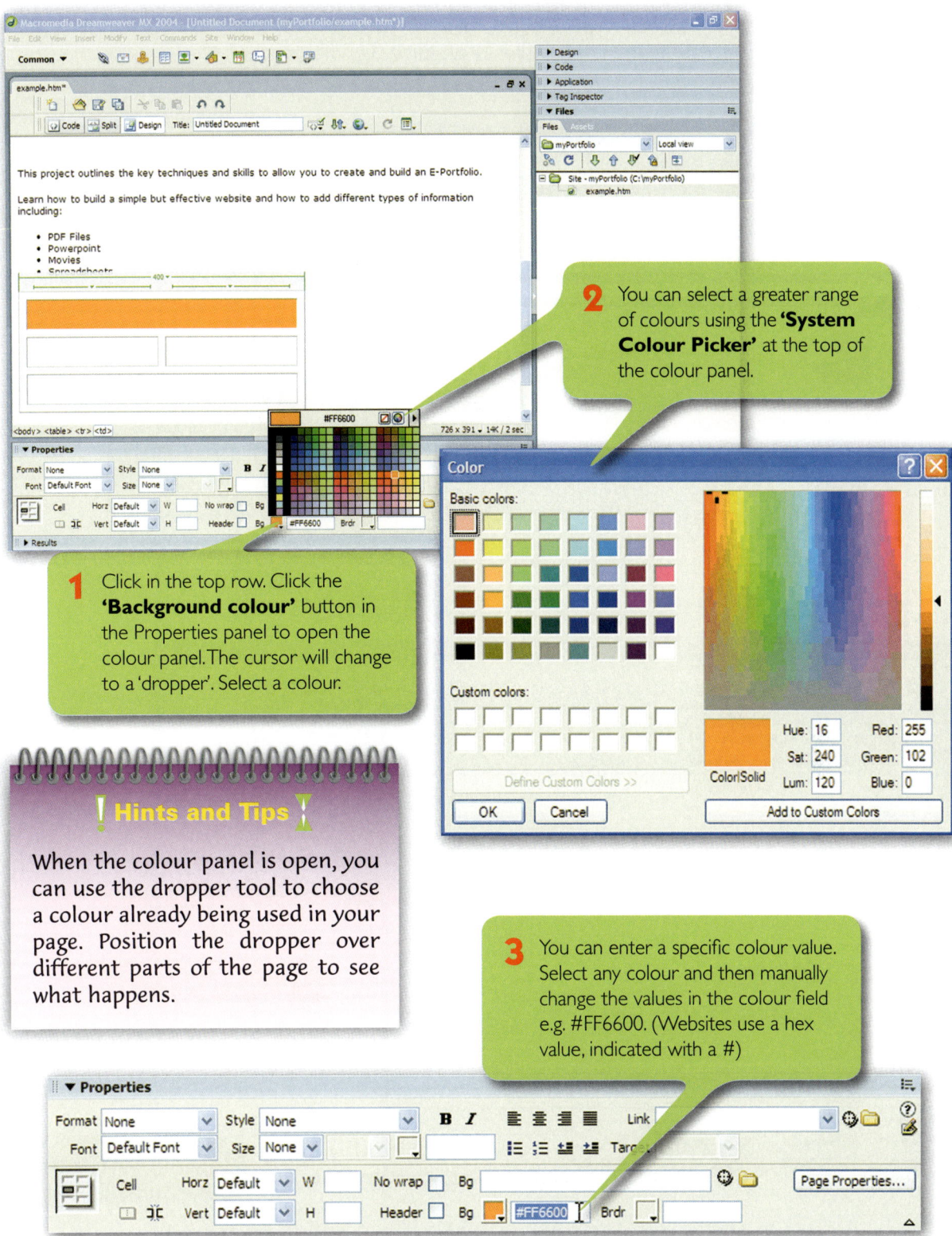

2 You can select a greater range of colours using the **'System Colour Picker'** at the top of the colour panel.

1 Click in the top row. Click the **'Background colour'** button in the Properties panel to open the colour panel. The cursor will change to a 'dropper'. Select a colour.

! Hints and Tips !

When the colour panel is open, you can use the dropper tool to choose a colour already being used in your page. Position the dropper over different parts of the page to see what happens.

3 You can enter a specific colour value. Select any colour and then manually change the values in the colour field e.g. #FF6600. (Websites use a hex value, indicated with a #)

Add text to a table

When you want to put text into a table you can type it, copy and paste it from somewhere or import it from a saved file. To practice we will use the text you've already typed on your page.

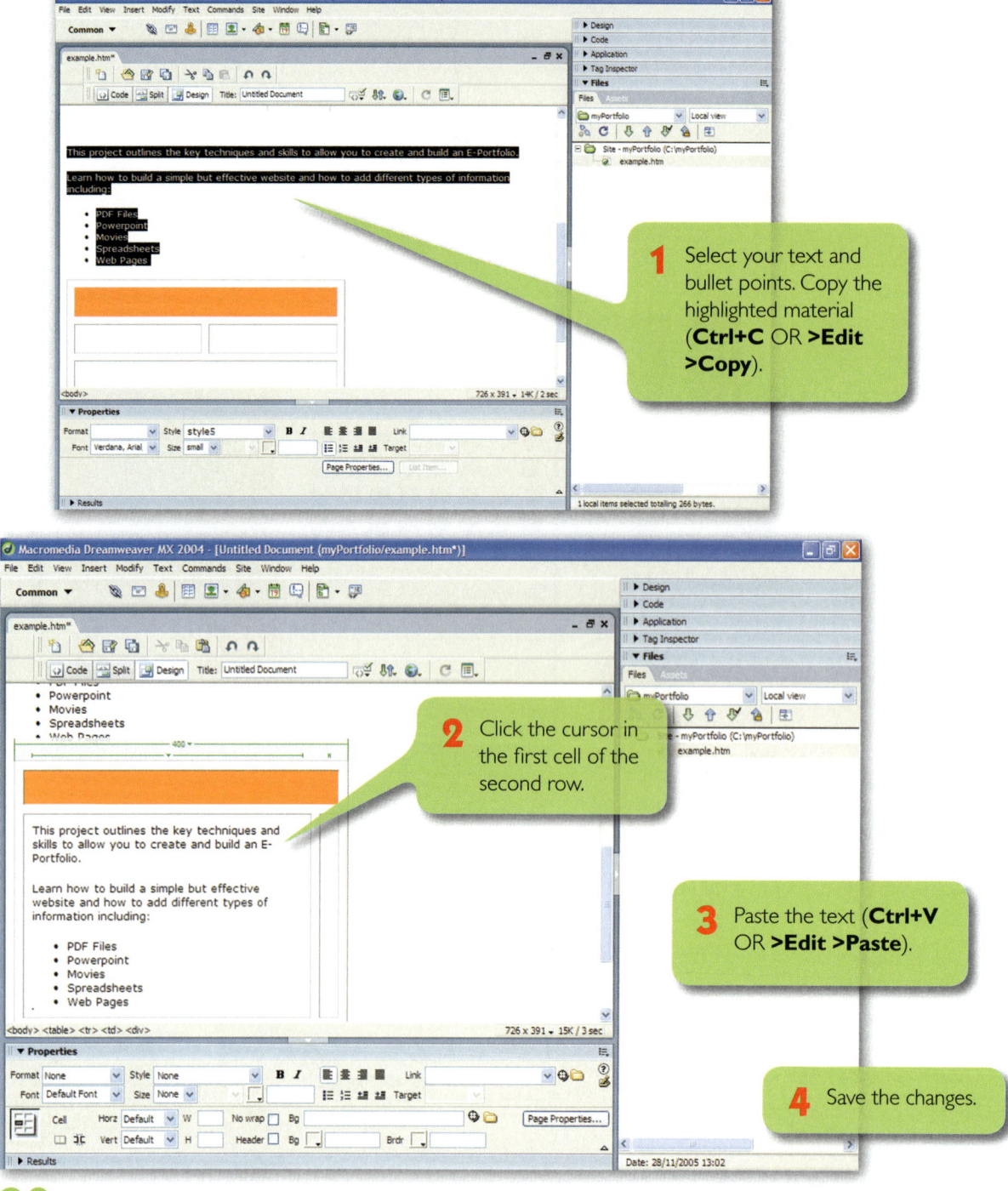

1 Select your text and bullet points. Copy the highlighted material (**Ctrl+C** OR **>Edit >Copy**).

2 Click the cursor in the first cell of the second row.

3 Paste the text (**Ctrl+V** OR **>Edit >Paste**).

4 Save the changes.

Add a graphic to a table

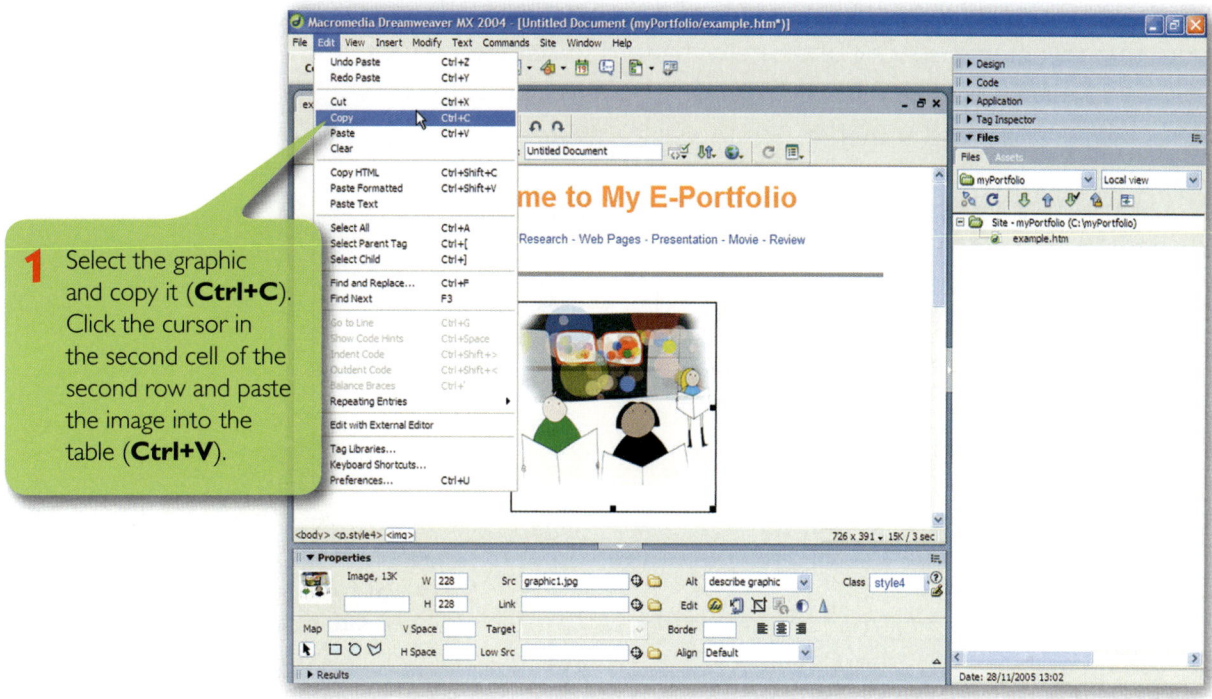

1 Select the graphic and copy it (**Ctrl+C**). Click the cursor in the second cell of the second row and paste the image into the table (**Ctrl+V**).

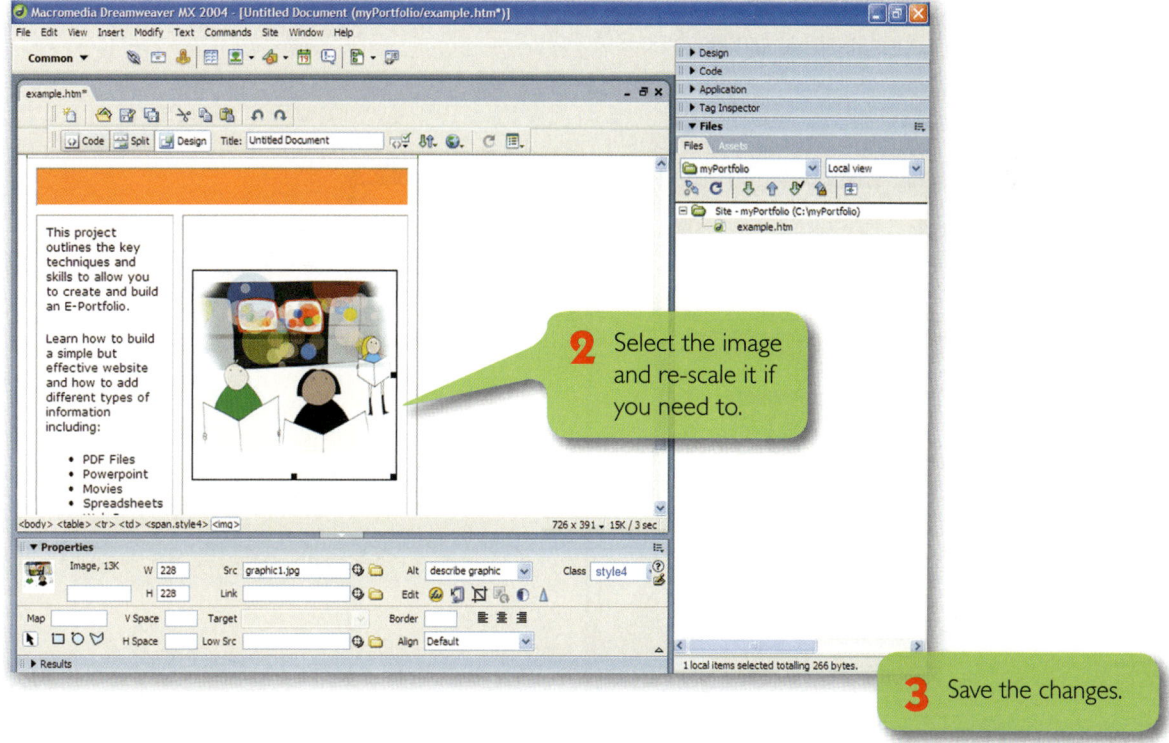

2 Select the image and re-scale it if you need to.

3 Save the changes.

Select and resize a table

The table you have created has a width of 400 pixels. As you added your text the internal spacing of the cells changed to suit the content. You can change the width of the table and the relative size of the cells and rows by dragging the internal row or cell borders.

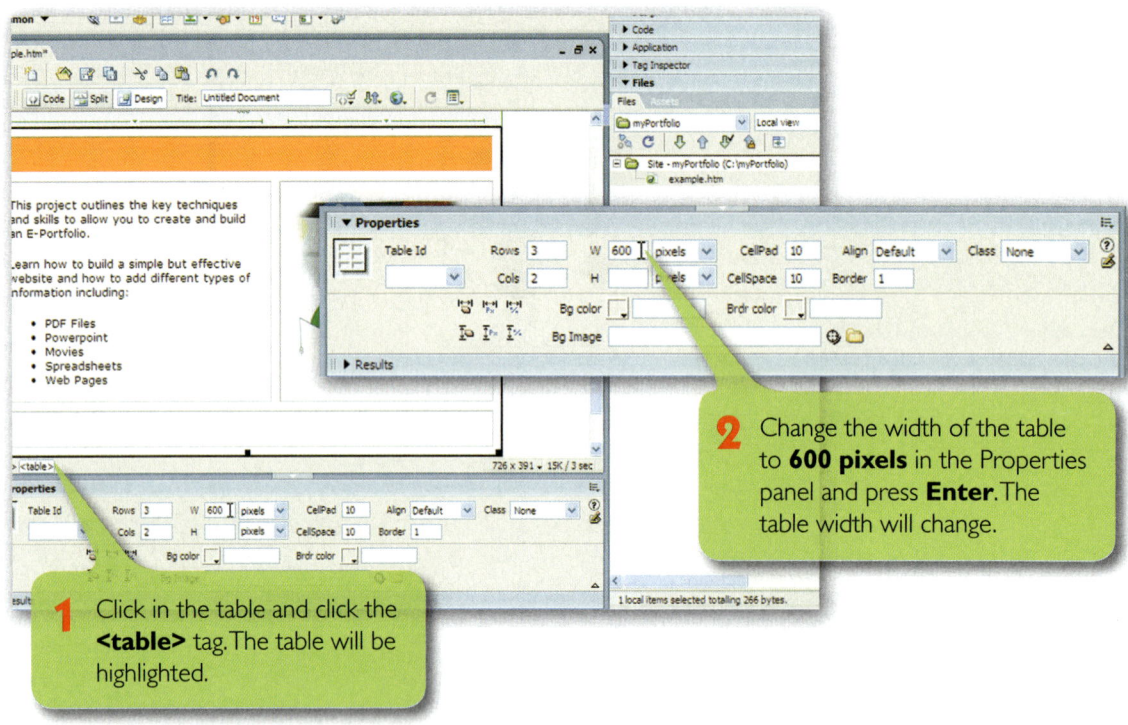

2 Change the width of the table to **600 pixels** in the Properties panel and press **Enter**. The table width will change.

1 Click in the table and click the **<table>** tag. The table will be highlighted.

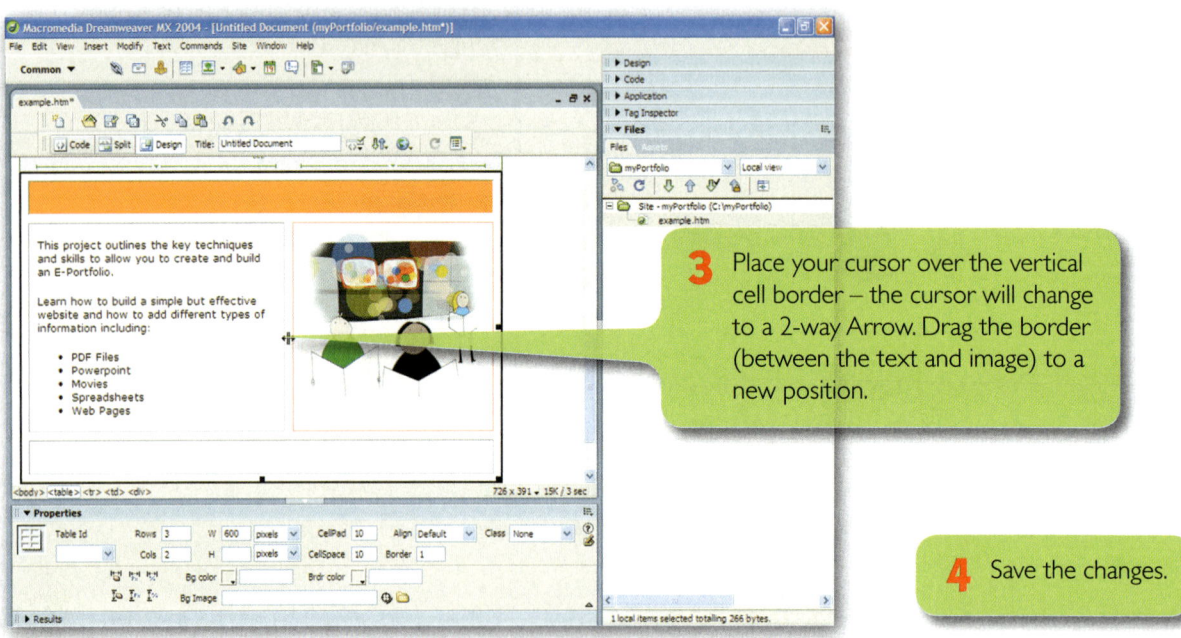

3 Place your cursor over the vertical cell border – the cursor will change to a 2-way Arrow. Drag the border (between the text and image) to a new position.

4 Save the changes.

Align items within a table

When you add text and images to a table the default settings are used to position the information. You can then align your text and images to suit your own design.

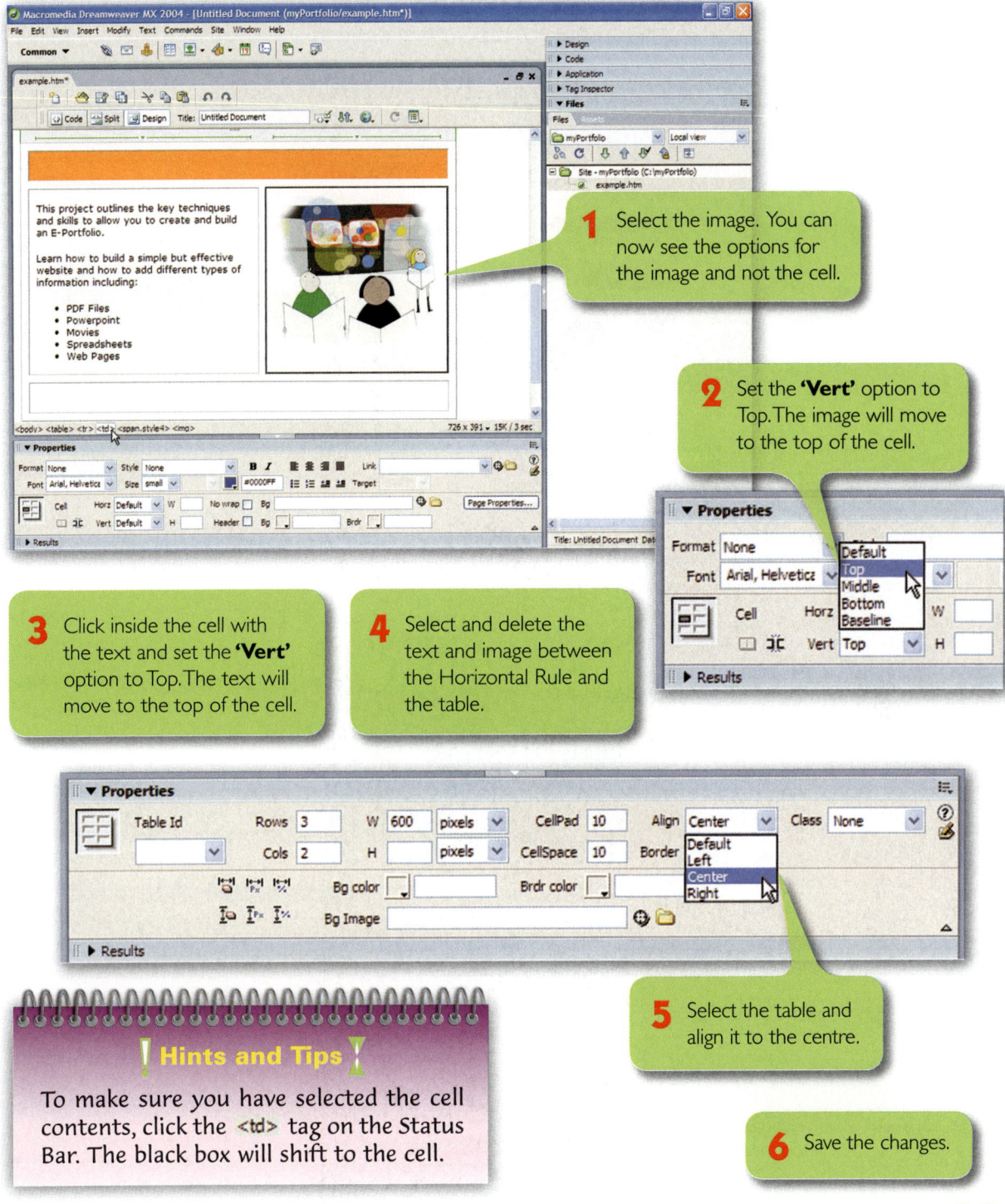

1 Select the image. You can now see the options for the image and not the cell.

2 Set the **'Vert'** option to Top. The image will move to the top of the cell.

3 Click inside the cell with the text and set the **'Vert'** option to Top. The text will move to the top of the cell.

4 Select and delete the text and image between the Horizontal Rule and the table.

5 Select the table and align it to the centre.

Hints and Tips

To make sure you have selected the cell contents, click the `<td>` tag on the Status Bar. The black box will shift to the cell.

6 Save the changes.

Use of special characters

When you are creating your E-portfolio you may need to use some special symbols like copyright, trademark or currency symbols. In Dreamweaver you need to use the special characters available on the Insert Bar. You also use the Insert Bar to create a new paragraph or a space.

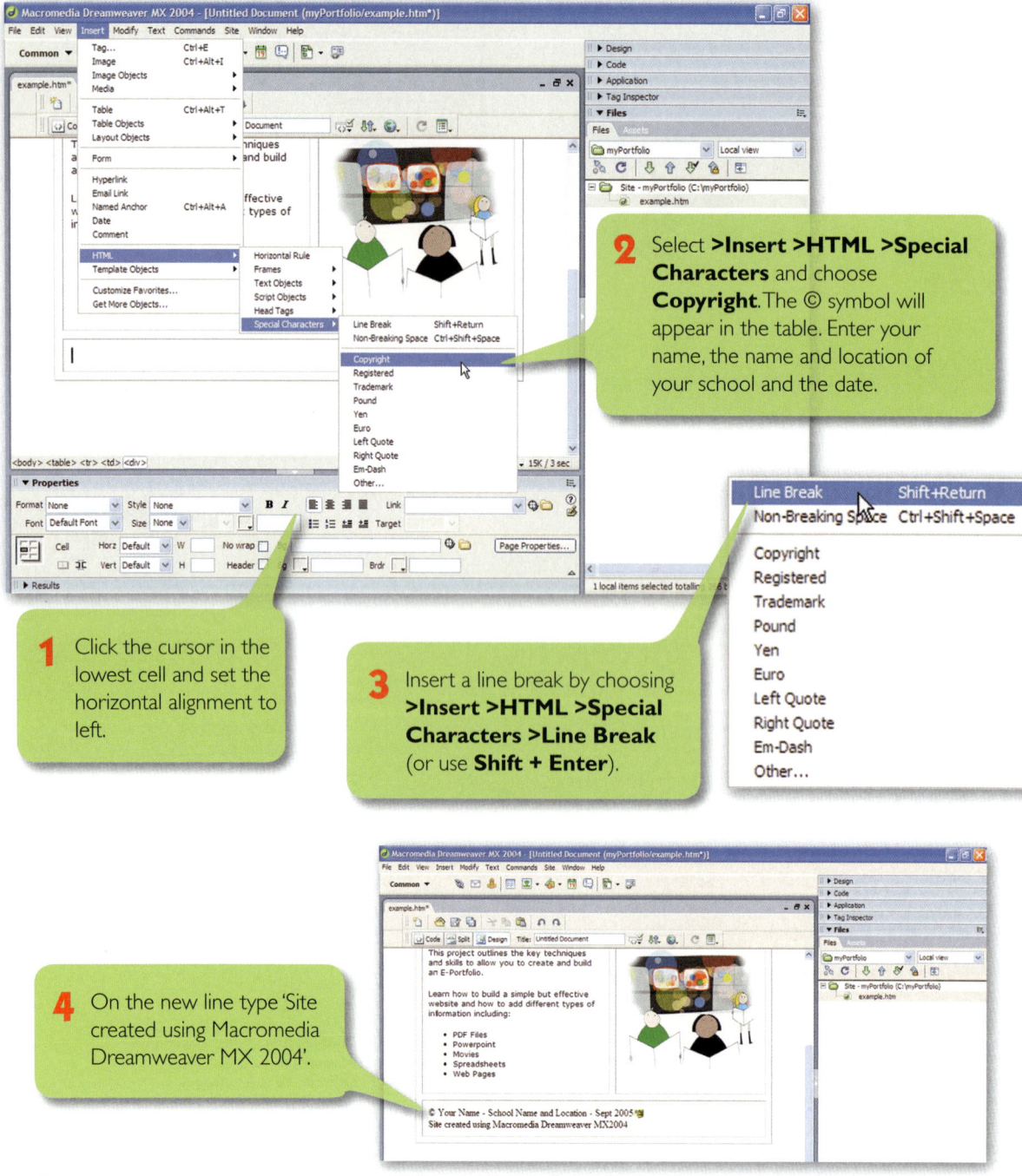

2 Select **>Insert >HTML >Special Characters** and choose **Copyright**. The © symbol will appear in the table. Enter your name, the name and location of your school and the date.

1 Click the cursor in the lowest cell and set the horizontal alignment to left.

3 Insert a line break by choosing **>Insert >HTML >Special Characters >Line Break** (or use **Shift + Enter**).

4 On the new line type 'Site created using Macromedia Dreamweaver MX 2004'.

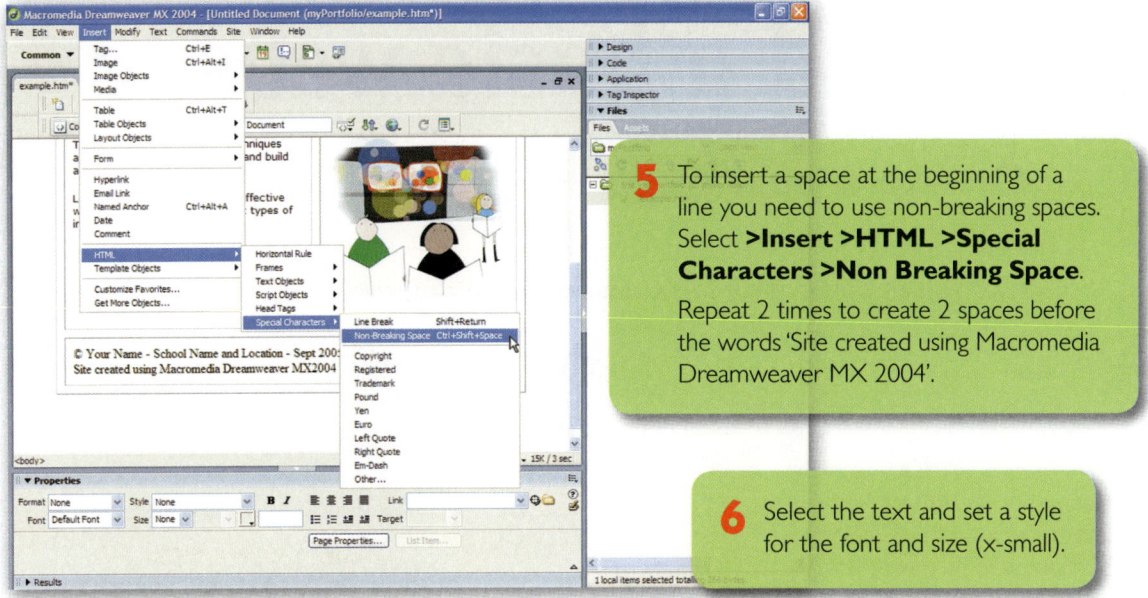

5 To insert a space at the beginning of a line you need to use non-breaking spaces. Select **>Insert >HTML >Special Characters >Non Breaking Space**.

Repeat 2 times to create 2 spaces before the words 'Site created using Macromedia Dreamweaver MX 2004'.

6 Select the text and set a style for the font and size (x-small).

7 Save the page **(Ctrl+S)** and preview the page in a browser **(F12)**.

Over to you

You can use the skills and ideas from this chapter to design the pages for your own E-portfolio to showcase your Food Matters! work.

You should have created a structure diagram for the E-portfolio. The next stage in creating an E-portfolio is to create storyboards for your pages.

Each page in your E-portfolio will have its own purpose but it is important that the pages work together. There are marks for including commentaries about your evidence and for a consistent approach to the design of your pages.

When you are creating your storyboards you will need to think about:

● How many pages you will need.
● Whether there things that you will need to include on every page.
● How you will lay out the pages.
● How the pages will link together.
● Accessibility issues.

You will need a home page to introduce your E-portfolio and you will also need menu and context pages. Pages 144 to 146 of the Student Book give you all the information that you will need. Create storyboards for your Food Matters! E-portfolio.

Use pages 101 and 102 of the Student Book to help you.

Hints and Tips

If you resize the browser window the table will remain a fixed size but the rest of the information will flow to fit the space available. Using tables will help you control the way your page looks.

4 Build a basic website

Create a new page

The first page of your E-portfolio acts as your 'home page'. This page gives you an opportunity to introduce your work for your SPB.

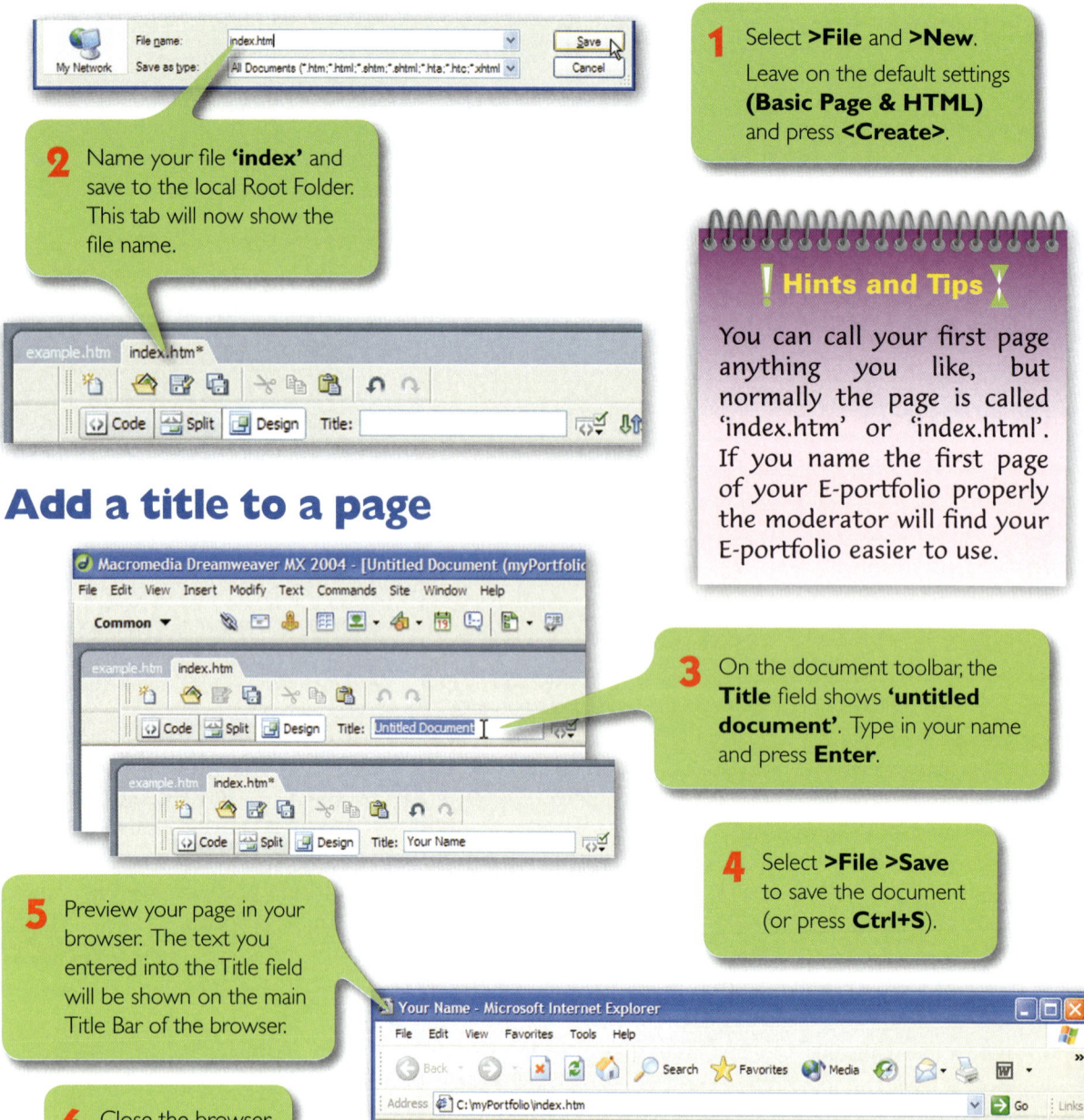

1 Select **>File** and **>New**. Leave on the default settings **(Basic Page & HTML)** and press **<Create>**.

2 Name your file **'index'** and save to the local Root Folder. This tab will now show the file name.

! Hints and Tips !

You can call your first page anything you like, but normally the page is called 'index.htm' or 'index.html'. If you name the first page of your E-portfolio properly the moderator will find your E-portfolio easier to use.

Add a title to a page

3 On the document toolbar, the **Title** field shows **'untitled document'**. Type in your name and press **Enter**.

4 Select **>File >Save** to save the document (or press **Ctrl+S**).

5 Preview your page in your browser. The text you entered into the Title field will be shown on the main Title Bar of the browser.

6 Close the browser.

Set the page properties

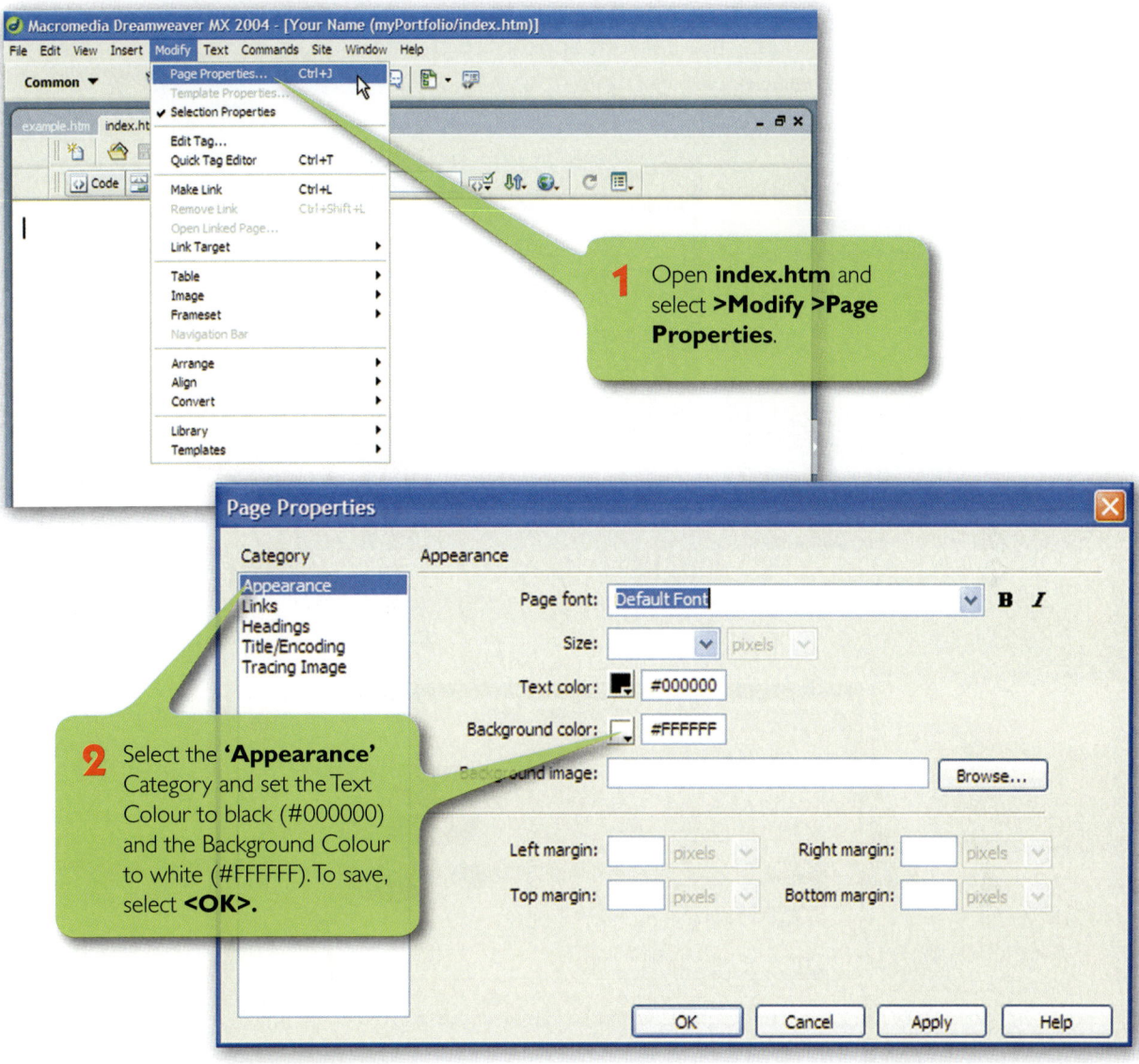

1 Open **index.htm** and select **>Modify >Page Properties**.

2 Select the **'Appearance'** Category and set the Text Colour to black (#000000) and the Background Colour to white (#FFFFFF). To save, select **<OK>.**

3 Select **>File >Save** to save the document.

! Hints and Tips !

Setting the page properties only sets the properties for that single page. The page will have the background and text colour of your choice, regardless of the browser it is viewed in. If you don't set these properties your audience may not see the page as you intended.

Layout a page using a table

Using a table gives you more control over the look of the page. When the table edges are 'invisible' the content appears to be laid out in a structured and ordered way.

2 Merge the cells in rows 1, 2, 3, 4 and 6 using this icon in the Properties panel. See page 28.

1 Click the cursor inside the **'index. htm'** page. Check that the Insert Panel is set to **'Common'** and choose the **'Insert Table'** icon.

Use these settings:
- Rows – 6
- Columns – 3
- Table Width – 600 Pixels
- Border Thickness – 0
- Cell Padding – 0
- Cell Spacing – 2

Select **<OK>**.

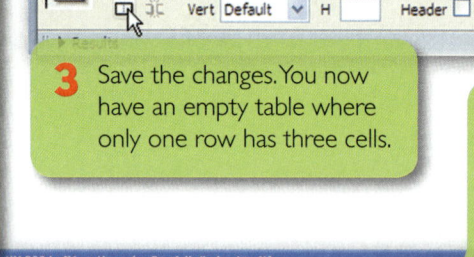

3 Save the changes. You now have an empty table where only one row has three cells.

5 Enter the text shown in each cell. Use the **'unordered list'** icon to convert the text list in Row 5 into bullet points.

4 Type 'Welcome to My E-Portfolio'.

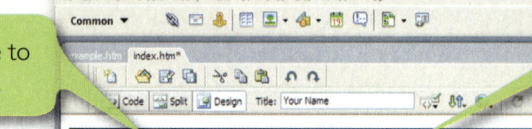

10 Save the changes.

6 Reposition the dividers as shown on page 32.

7 Click the cursor in the third cell of Row 5 and insert an image. Resize if required.

9 Click the cursor in Row 1 and set a background colour – #2D8A3D.

8 Use the Properties panel to align the text and image in Row 5 so both are **Vert: Top**.

! Hints and Tips !

Setting the table width to 'pixels' provides a fixed dimension and keeps the table the right width, so your audience sees the page as you intended. A pixel width up to 700 generally ensures your pages fit on A4 'portrait' paper.

Cell padding sets the spacing between the content and the borders of your table. Your cell padding is set to 0 at the moment. Change the value to see what happens - remember to set the value back to 0.

Add cells or rows

Once you have created and tested the prototype of your web page you may need to alter the table you are going to use to include more information.

1 Click the cursor in the second row (Home – Planning etc).

2 Select **>Insert > Table Objects** and choose the **'Insert Row Below'** option to add a new row. Click the cursor in this row.

3 Change the Insert Panel from **Common** view to **HTML** view.

4 Click the **Insert Horizontal Rule** icon and set the attributes of the rule in the Properties Panel to:
- Height – I
- Shading – off

5 Save the changes.

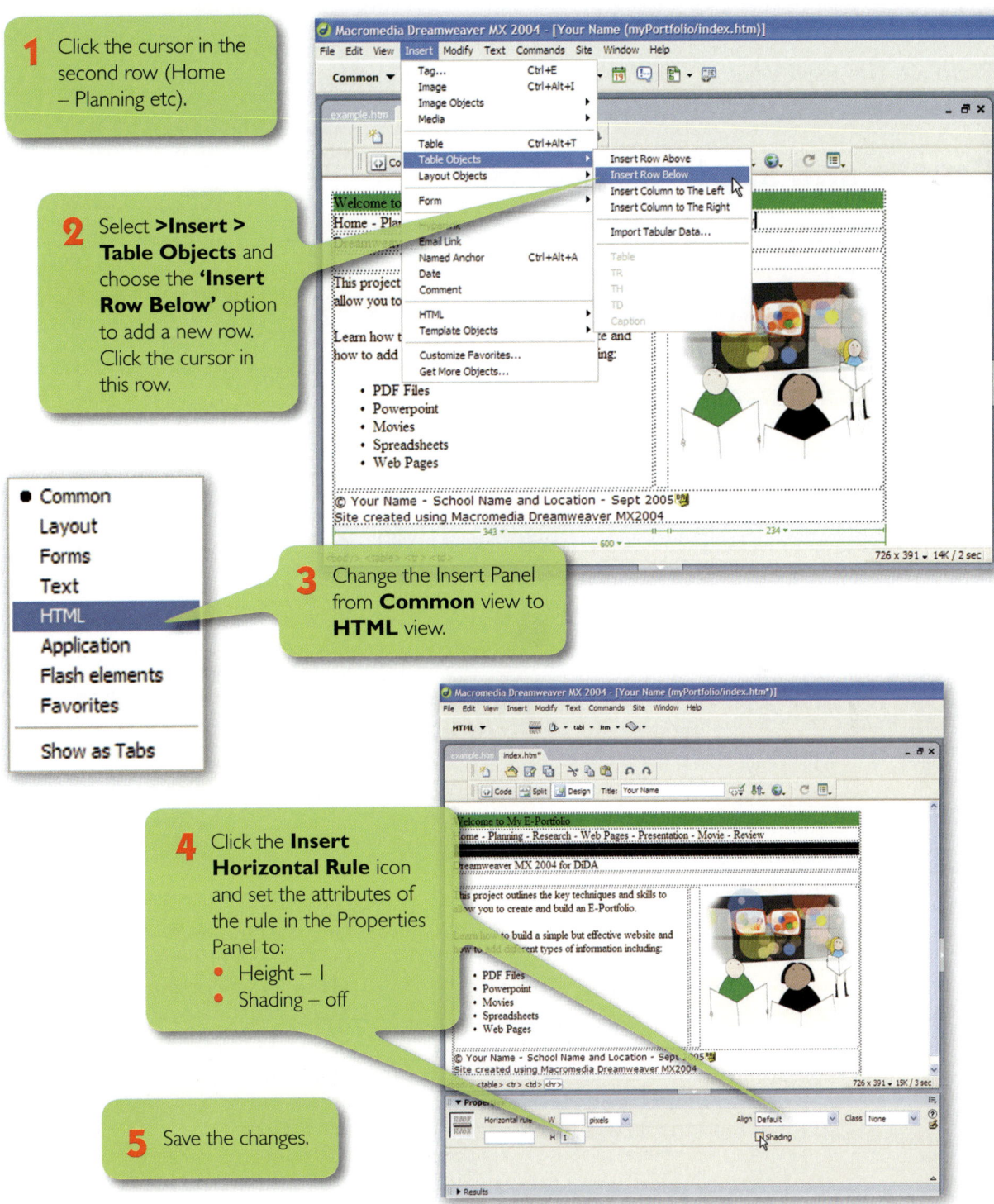

Cascading style sheets

You can use Cascading Style Sheets (CSS) to set up styles to apply to the content of your website. If you decide to change the style at a later date, you only need to change the CSS – the style will then be updated throughout your site.

There are two main types of CSS Styles – **Tag Styles** and **Class Rules**. They are created and selected using the CSS Styles Panel.

Create and apply a tag style

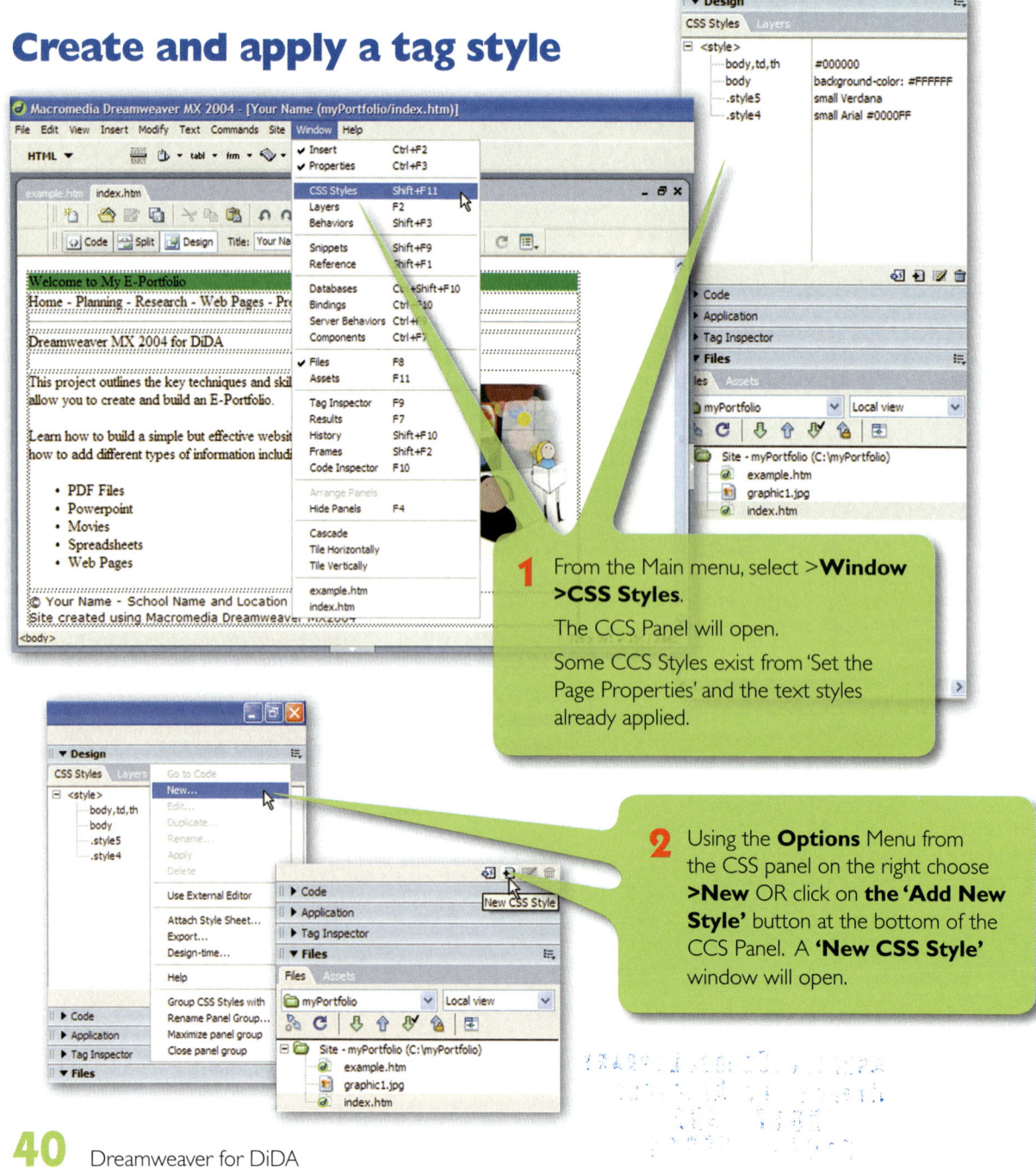

1 From the Main menu, select >**Window** >**CSS Styles**.

The CCS Panel will open.

Some CCS Styles exist from 'Set the Page Properties' and the text styles already applied.

2 Using the **Options** Menu from the CSS panel on the right choose >**New** OR click on **the 'Add New Style'** button at the bottom of the CCS Panel. A **'New CSS Style'** window will open.

3 Select the **<h1>** option from the Tag menu and the Tag option under **'Selector Type'**. Choose **'This Document Only'** and select **<OK>**. A window for **'Set the CSS Style Definition for h1'** will open.

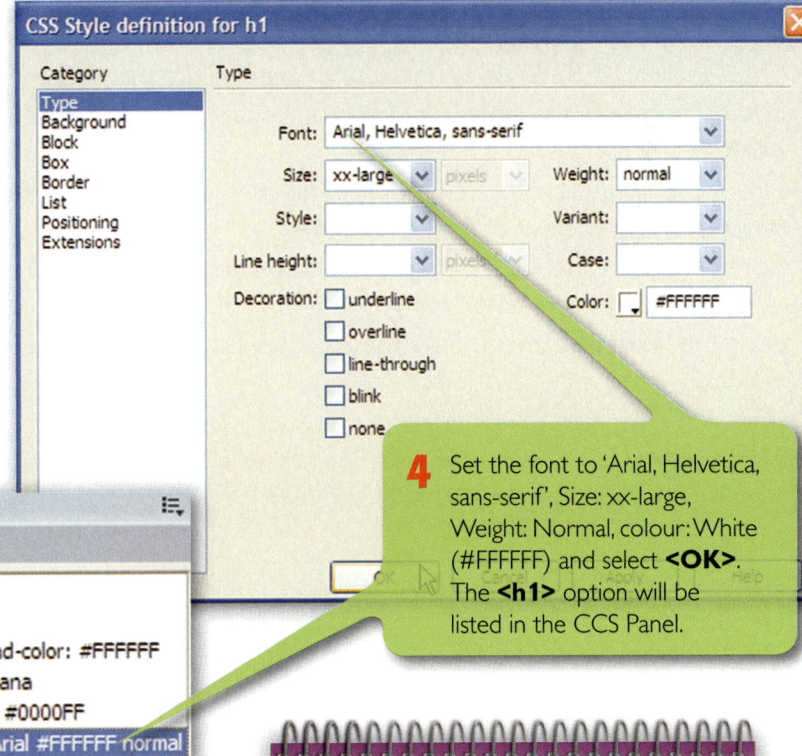

4 Set the font to 'Arial, Helvetica, sans-serif', Size: xx-large, Weight: Normal, colour: White (#FFFFFF) and select **<OK>**. The **<h1>** option will be listed in the CCS Panel.

▼ Design

CSS Styles	Layers

☐ <style>	
body,td,th	#000000
body	background-color: #FFFFFF
.style5	small Verdana
.style4	small Arial #0000FF
h1	xx-large Arial #FFFFFF normal

Apply the tag style to format the text

- Click anywhere within the text 'Welcome to My E-Portfolio'.
- Click on the **'Format'** menu and select **'Heading 1'** – the text will change to show the new settings.
- Save the changes.

Duplicate and change a tag style

You will need to set different **Tag Styles** for different headings and content in your table. The easiest way to do this, especially if the same font is to be used each time is to duplicate the original tag style and edit the details.

- Select the **<h1>** option in the CSS Panel. Right-click on the selected tag and choose **'Duplicate'**.
- The 'Duplicate CSS Style' window will open. Select the **<h2>** option in the Tag menu (the other settings will remain the same) and select **<OK>**.
- Select and right-click the new option. This time choose **'Edit'**. Set the styles as shown below and select **<OK>**.
- Repeat steps 1-3 to create each of the tag styles shown below.
- When finished select each text group and apply the appropriate style using the **'Format'** menu. Save the changes and preview in a browser window.

<h2> Navigation	Font: Arial, Helvetica, Sans-serif Size: small Weight: Normal Colour: #0000FF (blue)
<h3> Page Title	Font: Arial, Helvetica, Sans-serif Size: xx-large Weight: Bold Colour: #333366 (dark blue)
<p> Paragraph text	Font: Verdana, Arial, Helvetica, Sans-serif Size: small Weight: Normal Colour: #000000 (black)
<h4> Footer	Font: Verdana, Arial, Helvetica, Sans-serif Size: xx-small Weight: Normal Colour: #666666 (grey)

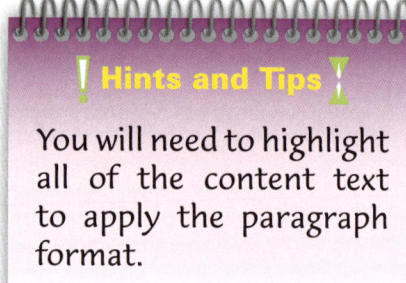

Hints and Tips

You will need to highlight all of the content text to apply the paragraph format.

Create a class rule

When you design your web pages you may decide to apply a specific look to a certain word, perhaps to emphasise it. This is done by applying a **Class Rule**.

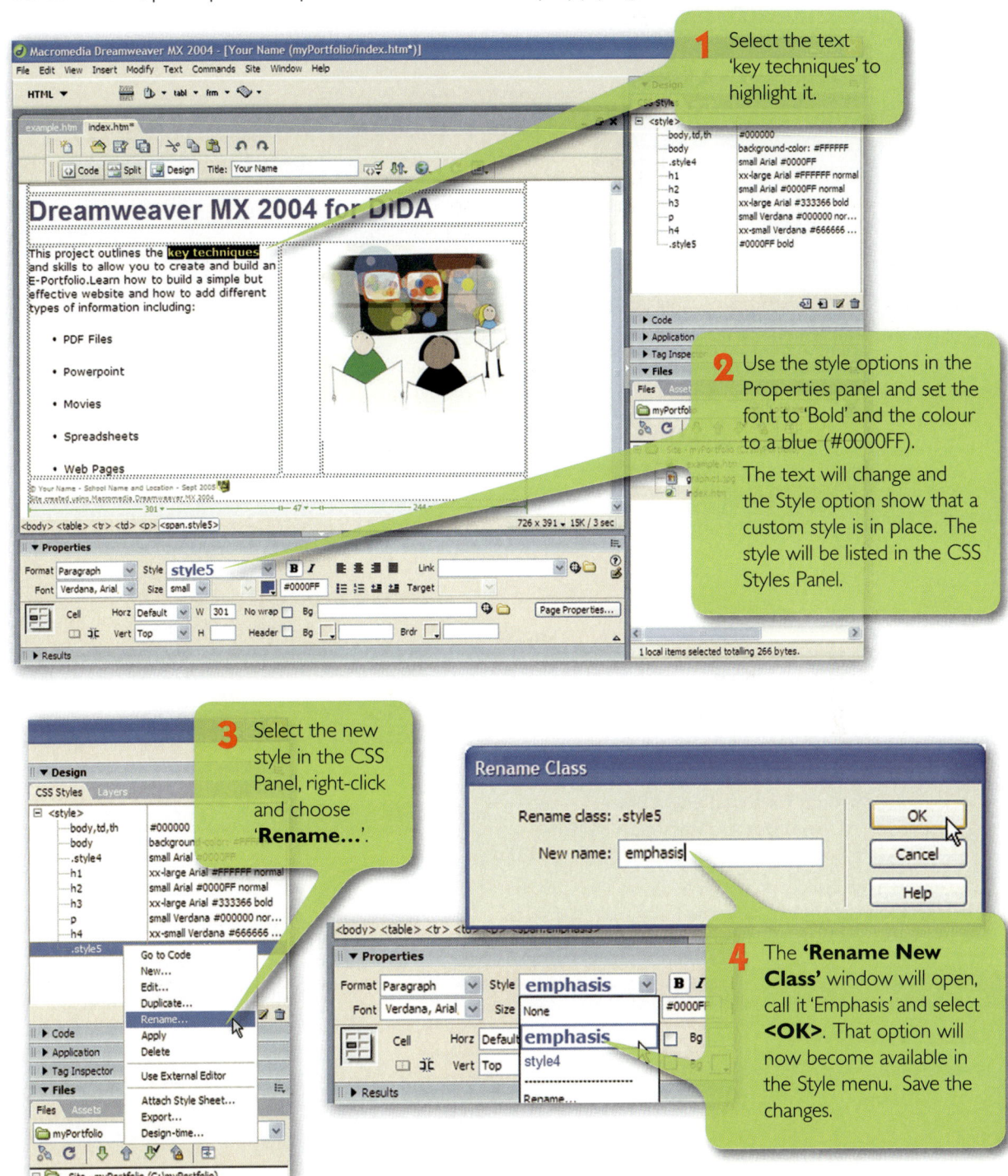

1 Select the text 'key techniques' to highlight it.

2 Use the style options in the Properties panel and set the font to 'Bold' and the colour to a blue (#0000FF).

The text will change and the Style option show that a custom style is in place. The style will be listed in the CSS Styles Panel.

3 Select the new style in the CSS Panel, right-click and choose '**Rename...**'.

4 The '**Rename New Class**' window will open, call it 'Emphasis' and select **<OK>**. That option will now become available in the Style menu. Save the changes.

Create an external style sheet

To create a style that can be used on more than one page of your website you need to create an External Style Sheet. This is useful for setting up your E-portfolio as you will want the style to be consistent.

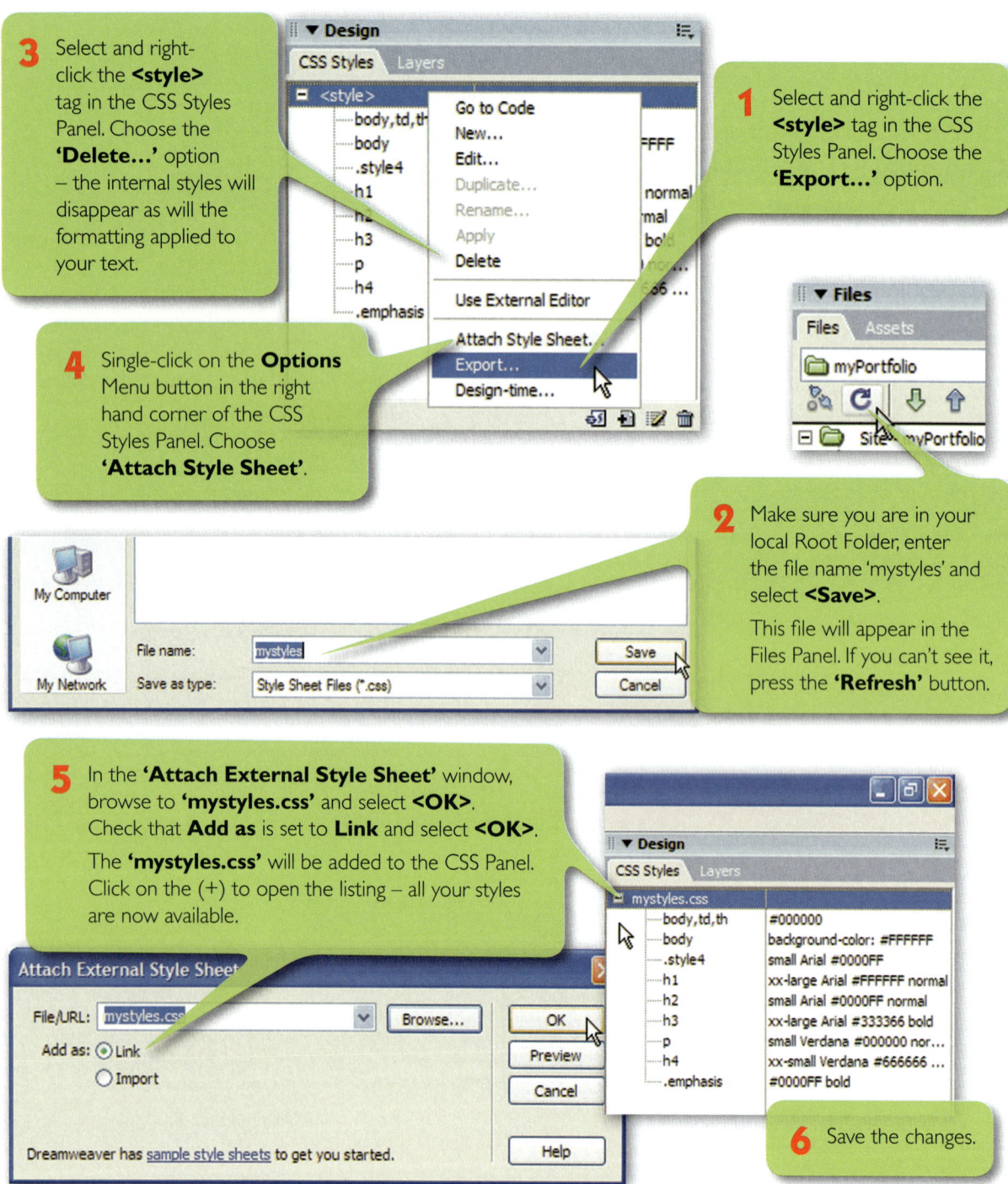

3 Select and right-click the **<style>** tag in the CSS Styles Panel. Choose the **'Delete...'** option – the internal styles will disappear as will the formatting applied to your text.

1 Select and right-click the **<style>** tag in the CSS Styles Panel. Choose the **'Export...'** option.

4 Single-click on the **Options** Menu button in the right hand corner of the CSS Styles Panel. Choose **'Attach Style Sheet'**.

2 Make sure you are in your local Root Folder, enter the file name 'mystyles' and select **<Save>**.

This file will appear in the Files Panel. If you can't see it, press the **'Refresh'** button.

5 In the **'Attach External Style Sheet'** window, browse to **'mystyles.css'** and select **<OK>**. Check that **Add as** is set to **Link** and select **<OK>**.

The **'mystyles.css'** will be added to the CSS Panel. Click on the (+) to open the listing – all your styles are now available.

6 Save the changes.

Create a template

When you design your E-portfolio you may have many pages that share certain features such as a common layout for the header bar, menu structure, page titles etc. Instead of having to create a layout for each page you can use a template to create a 'master' page and then duplicate it to create the other pages. If you make changes to the 'master' template then the other pages will be automatically changed.

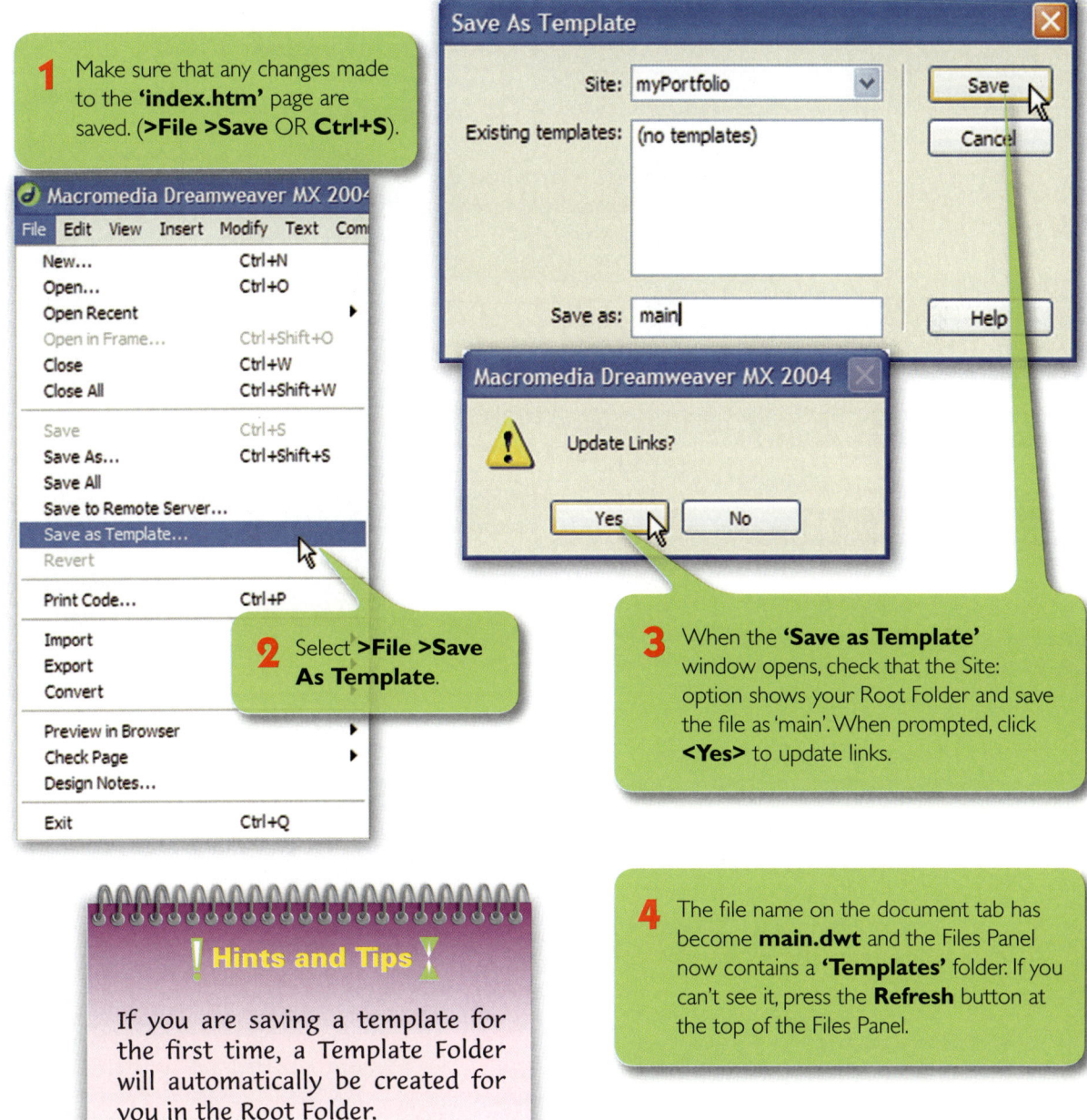

1 Make sure that any changes made to the **'index.htm'** page are saved. (**>File >Save** OR **Ctrl+S**).

2 Select **>File >Save As Template**.

3 When the **'Save as Template'** window opens, check that the Site: option shows your Root Folder and save the file as 'main'. When prompted, click **<Yes>** to update links.

4 The file name on the document tab has become **main.dwt** and the Files Panel now contains a **'Templates'** folder. If you can't see it, press the **Refresh** button at the top of the Files Panel.

⏳ Hints and Tips ⏳

If you are saving a template for the first time, a Template Folder will automatically be created for you in the Root Folder.

Define an editable region

Once you have created a template, you can define what areas of the page can be edited and which remain fixed.

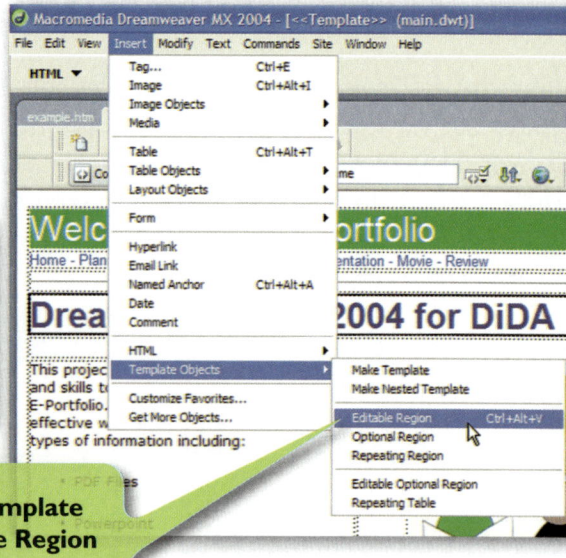

1 Open **'main.dwt'**. Click the cursor inside an area you want to make editable, for example the 'Page Title' – 'Dreamweaver MX 2004 for DiDA'.

2 Click the **<td>** tag in the Tag Selector to specifically select that area.

3 Select **>Insert >Template Objects >Editable Region** from the main menu bar.

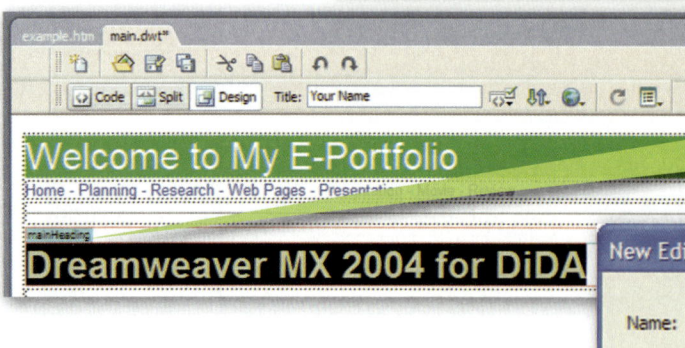

4 Name it 'mainHeading' and click **<OK>**. The editable region will be bounded by a rectangular box and identified with a named tab.

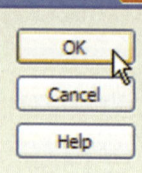

5 Repeat for other editable areas:
- Click the cursor inside the empty cell below and click the **<td>** tag to select.
- Select **>Insert >Template Objects >Editable Region**, name it 'mainContent1' and click **<OK>**.
- Click the cursor inside the area containing the text 'This project outlines....' and click the **<td>** tag to select.
- Select **>Insert >Template Objects >Editable Region**, name it 'mainContent2' and click **<OK>**
- Click inside the area containing the image and click the **<td>** tag.
- Select **>Insert >Template Objects >Editable Region**, name it 'mainImage' and click **<OK>**.

6 Delete the content from inside each of the editable regions and save the .dwt file. Do not 'Save as Template' – just 'Save'. It already is a Template.

7 Close the **'main.dwt'** document.

Create a page from a template

You have now created a template from your original page 'index.htm'. This will form the starting point for the other pages of your E-portfolio. To help demonstrate how templates work we will first make a copy of the original 'index' file so it can be used as a reference later on.

1 Check the **'index.htm'** document window is closed and then select **'index.htm'** in the Files Panel and right-click.

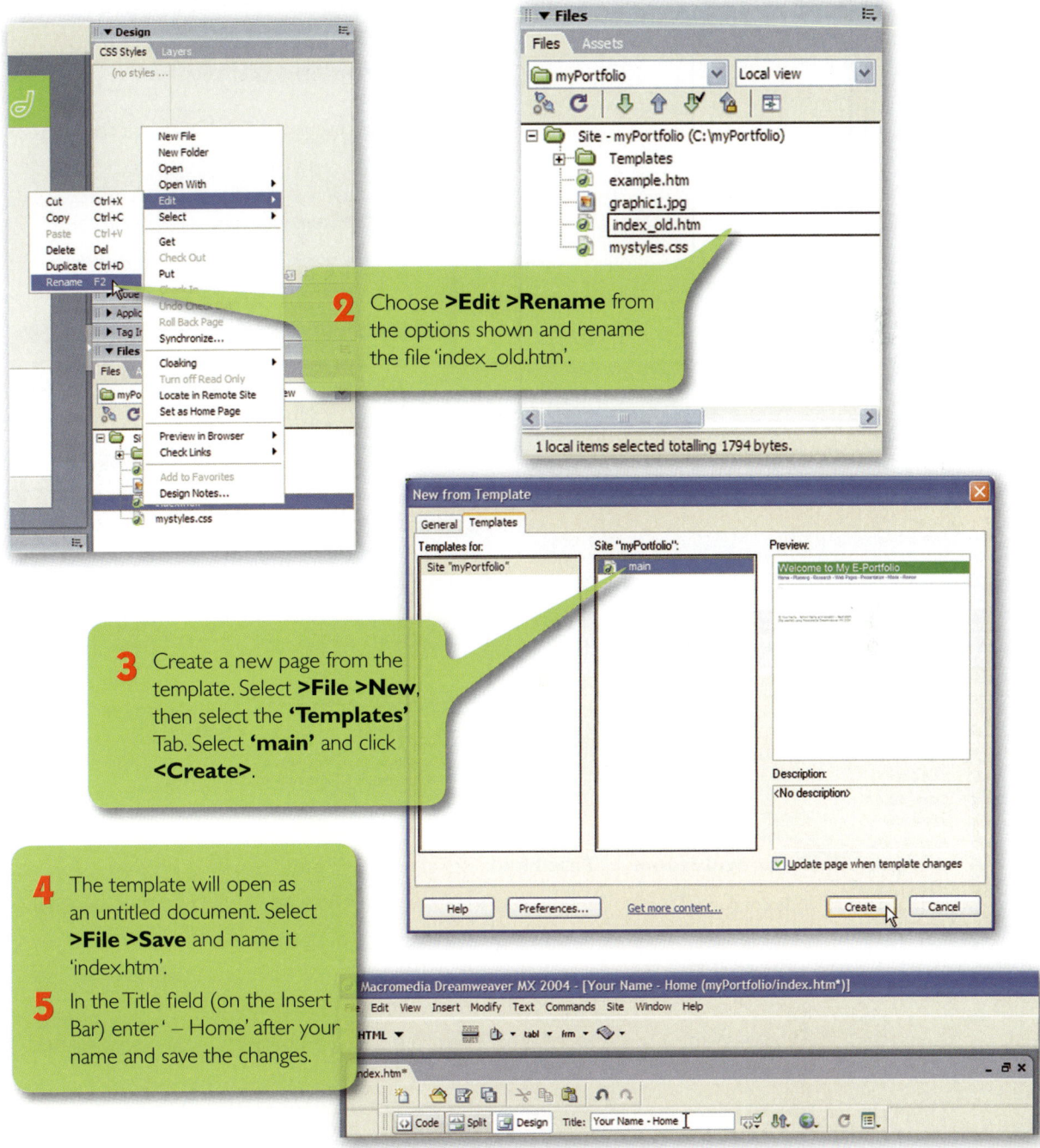

2 Choose **>Edit >Rename** from the options shown and rename the file 'index_old.htm'.

3 Create a new page from the template. Select **>File >New**, then select the **'Templates'** Tab. Select **'main'** and click **<Create>**.

4 The template will open as an untitled document. Select **>File >Save** and name it 'index.htm'.

5 In the Title field (on the Insert Bar) enter ' – Home' after your name and save the changes.

Create and name multiple pages

You can use the template to create and name a series of blank pages, one for each section of your E-portfolio.

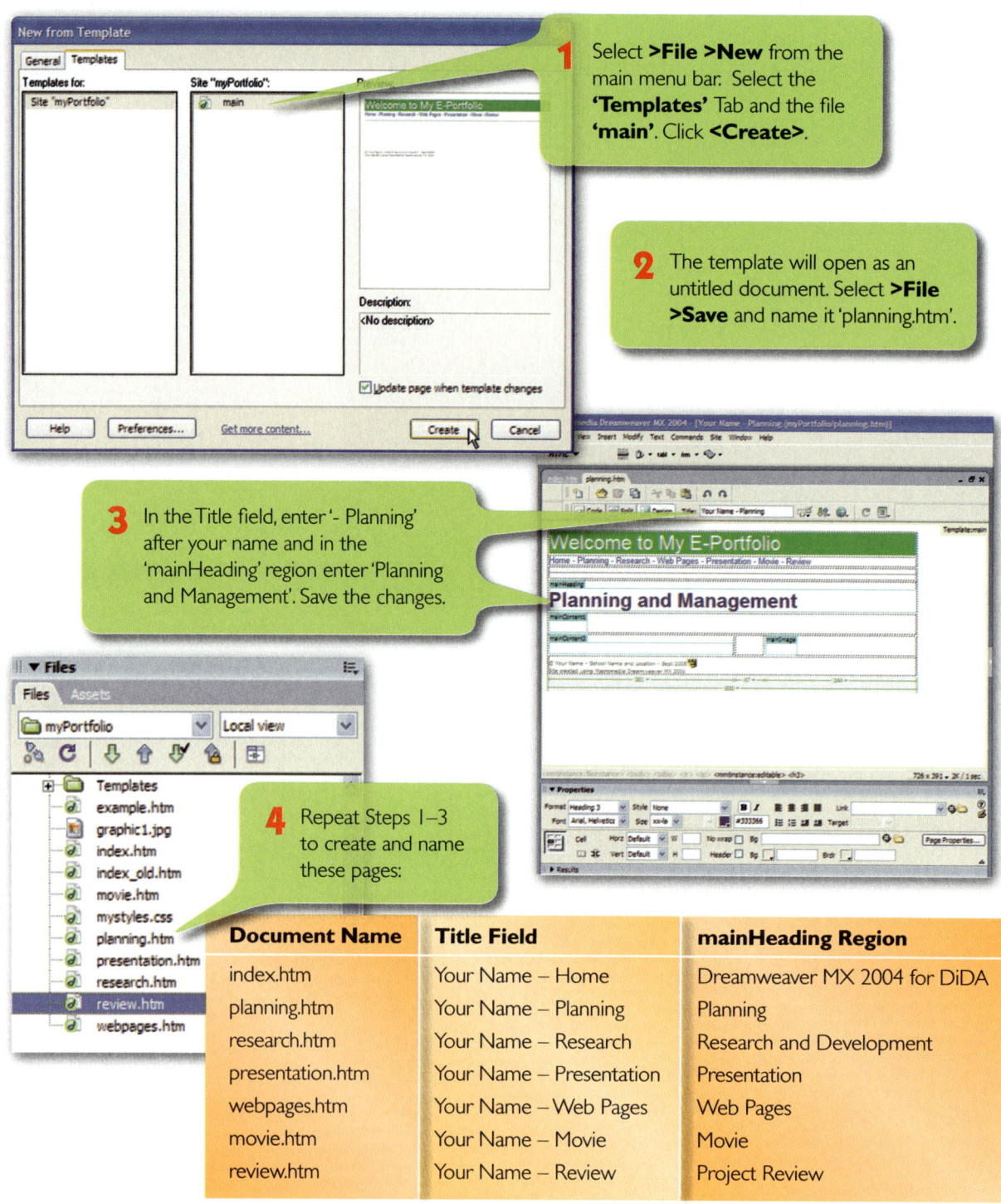

1 Select **>File >New** from the main menu bar. Select the **'Templates'** Tab and the file **'main'**. Click **<Create>**.

2 The template will open as an untitled document. Select **>File >Save** and name it 'planning.htm'.

3 In the Title field, enter '- Planning' after your name and in the 'mainHeading' region enter 'Planning and Management'. Save the changes.

4 Repeat Steps 1–3 to create and name these pages:

Document Name	Title Field	mainHeading Region
index.htm	Your Name – Home	Dreamweaver MX 2004 for DiDA
planning.htm	Your Name – Planning	Planning
research.htm	Your Name – Research	Research and Development
presentation.htm	Your Name – Presentation	Presentation
webpages.htm	Your Name – Web Pages	Web Pages
movie.htm	Your Name – Movie	Movie
review.htm	Your Name – Review	Project Review

Add navigation and links

The benefit of a website is that you can navigate through and around the pages to view the content. While you are developing a site, it is useful to prepare the interactive structure and key navigation early on then add content as you go along. This means that you can check that the navigation and content work and that the site is 'doing its job'.

Add internal links

1 Save and close all the open documents.

2 Open the **'main.dwt'** template.

3 Select and highlight the text 'Home' in the navigation bar. Make sure you can see the **'index.htm'** file in the Files Panel.

4 Position the cursor over the **'Point to File'** icon in the Properties panel. Click and drag the **'Point to File arrow'** to the **'index. htm'** file in the Files Panel. The link will become underlined and the path of the link will appear in the Link text box.

5 Repeat to add links for each of the remaining options (Planning, Research, Presentation, Web Pages, Movie and Review).

6 Select **>File >Save**. Dreamweaver will ask to update the other pages – select **<Yes>** and then **<Close>**.

7 Preview in the browser. You will now be able to navigate from one section to another.

Add an external link to a website

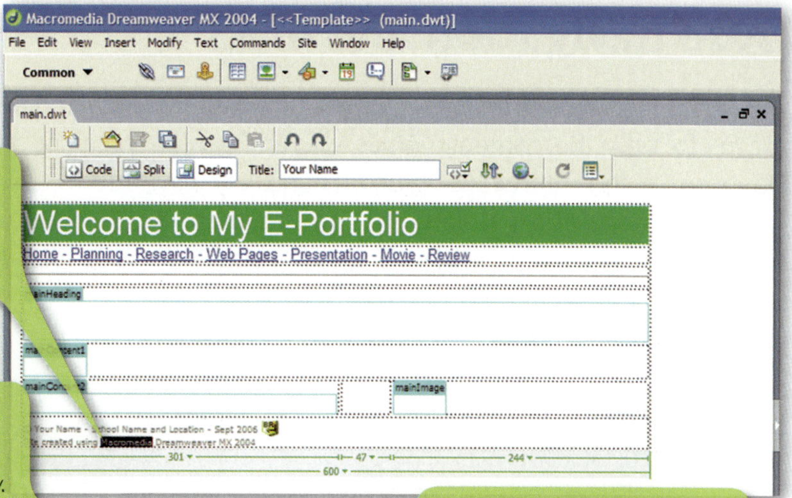

1 Open **'main.dwt'**. Select the text containing Macromedia in the footer bar.

2 Type http://www.macromedia.com into the **Link** field in the Property Inspector and press the Return key.

3 Select **'_Blank'** from the Target options. This will set the Macromedia website to open in a new browser window.

4 The appearance of the link will change. Save the template **'main.dwt'**, select **<Yes>** and then **<Close>**.

5 Preview the page in the browser. Click on the link to launch the website.

Add an email link

1 Open **'main.dwt'**. Select the text containing your name in the footer bar.

2 Type mailto: followed by the required email address into the **Link** option in the Properties panel. Make sure there are no spaces and press the **Return** key.

3 The appearance of the link will change. Save the template **'main.dwt'**, select **<Yes>** to the Update prompt and then **<Close>**.

4 Preview the page in the browser. Click on the link to launch the email window.

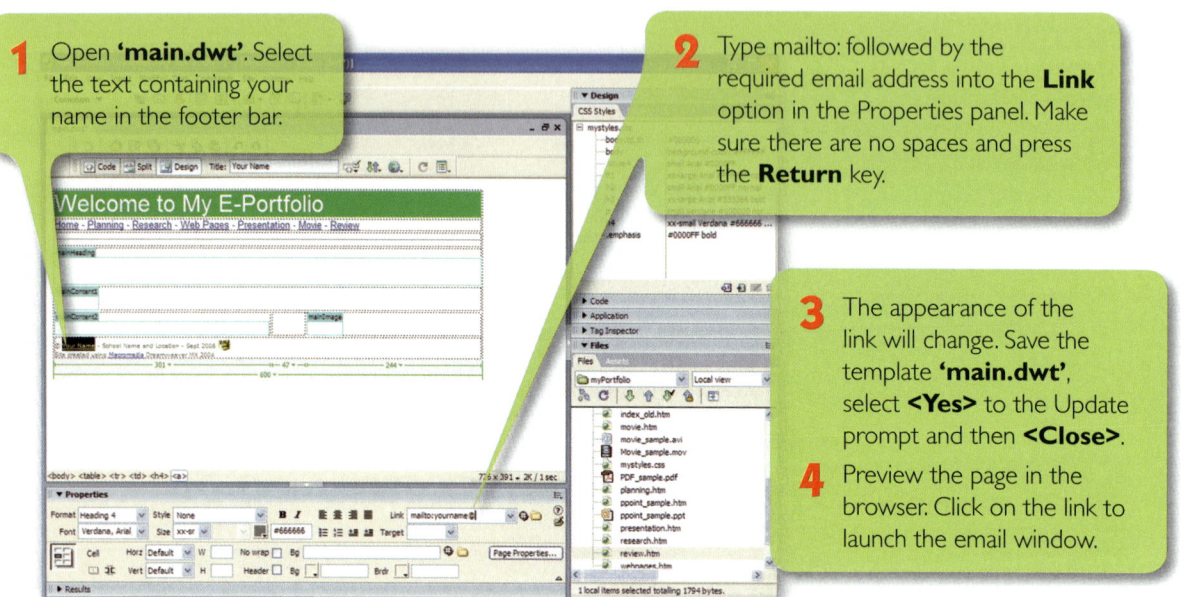

Use CSS to style links

You can add in some visual information to provide feedback to users as they navigate through the site.

This can be set up using Cascading Style Sheets. There are four options:

- **a:link** – the colour the user sees when they have not yet visted the target page of a link
- **a:visited** – the colour the link assumes once the user has visited a that target page
- **a:hover** – provides a rollover state that is activated when the cursor is positioned on that area (provides useful feedback as to what areas are 'live' and can be selected)
- **a:active** – the colour the user sees when they click a link

1 To create a link style select **>Window >CSS Styles**.

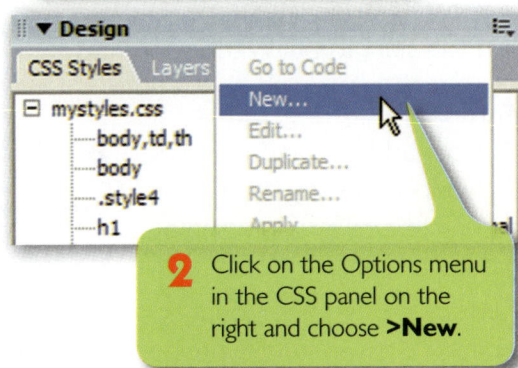

2 Click on the Options menu in the CSS panel on the right and choose **>New**.

3 Select the **Advanced** Selector Type and choose **'a:link'** from the selector drop down menu.

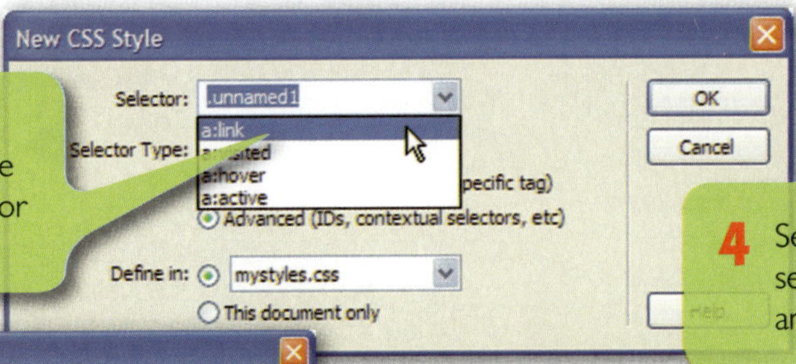

4 Select **Define in**: and set to **'myStyle.css'** and click **<OK>**.

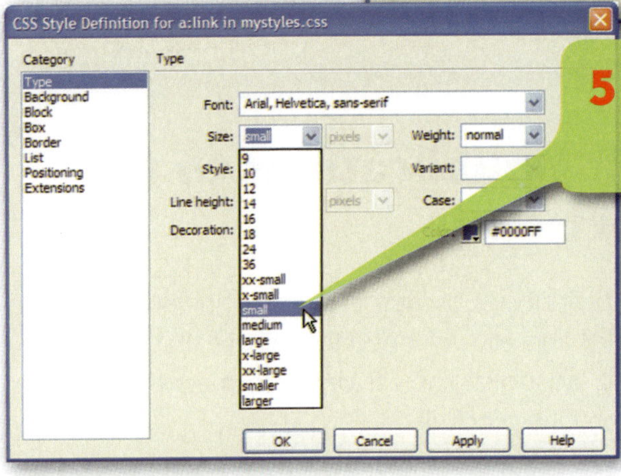

5 Choose the font type and style for the a:link (you can use the suggestions below).

6 Repeat for the Visited and Hover styles.

7 Preview **'index.htm'** in the browser. As the changes have not yet been saved for **'mystyles.css'**, a prompt will ask you to save. Select **<Yes>**. The new link states will be active.

<a:link>	Font: Arial, Helvetica, Sans-serif, Size: small Weight: Normal Decoration: Underline Text Colour: #0000FF (a blue)
<a:visited>	Font: Arial, Helvetica, Sans-serif, Size: small Weight: Normal Decoration: Underline Text Colour: #990066 (a purple)
<a:hover>	Font: Arial, Helvetica, Sans-serif, Size: small Weight: Normal Text Colour: #FFFFFF (white) Background colour: #000000 (black)

Import content

You've identified the audience for your E-portfolio as your teacher and the exam board's moderator. You must remember that the purpose of your E-portfolio is to showcase your publications and to give access to your supporting evidence. Once you've set up the structure of your E-portfolio, you can start to put in the content.

Add text and a graphic

You can add text and graphics to your pages by typing or pasting text or by importing or pasting an image.

Click inside the blue bounded 'Editable Region' and type or paste text or an image.

1 Click inside the blue bounded 'Editable Region' and type or paste text or an image.

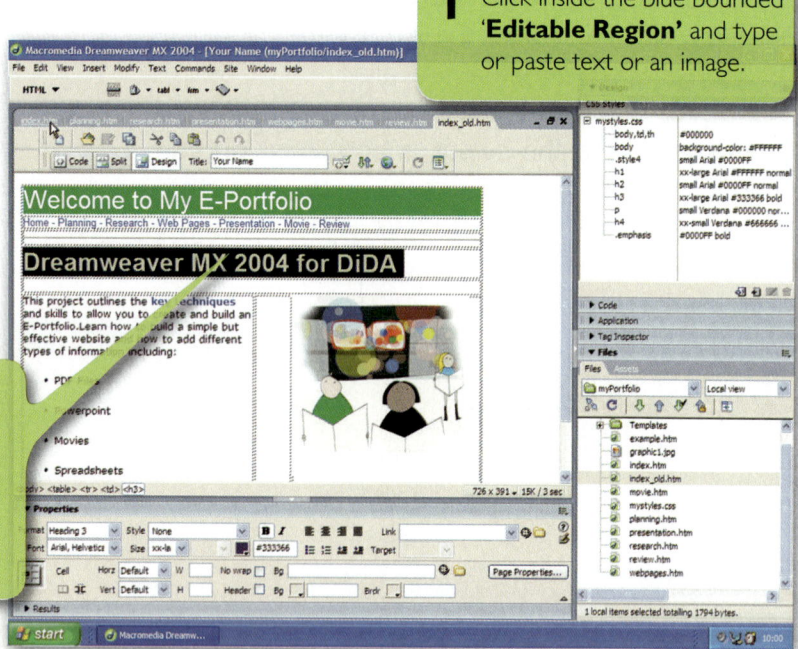

2 Open the file **'index_old.htm'** and copy the information from a single cell. Select **'index.htm'**, click inside the relevant blue bounded **'Editable Region'** and paste the content.

3 Repeat until all the content has been copied across. Save the file.

4 Close **'index_old.htm'**.

5 Go back to **'index.htm'** and try clicking on various parts of the page. You can now only change or select content held in the **'editable regions'**.

6 Save the file and preview in a browser – it should look the same as before.

7 Close the browser.

Adding publications to the E-portfolio

You will produce publications in lots of different formats for the SPB and you will need to prepare that work to go into the E-portfolio. The list of file formats that you can use will probably include:

- html, htm, xml
- pdf
- mov, avi, wmv
- jpg, png, gif, tif
- txt
- swf
- wav, midi, mp3
- pps, ppt

Using these file types will make sure that your teacher and your moderator can open all your work. You will need to convert some of your work to different formats to use it in your E-portfolio.

Import content from Word

You will have created supporting evidence and publications using word processing software. Sometimes you will want to save these publications as PDF documents to make sure that the formatting of the text is kept.

Sometimes you will want to add text to your web pages straight from your word processing application. These instructions show you how to do this.

1 Open the file in MS Word. If you only want to use some of the text, copy and paste the text into a new Word document and save it.

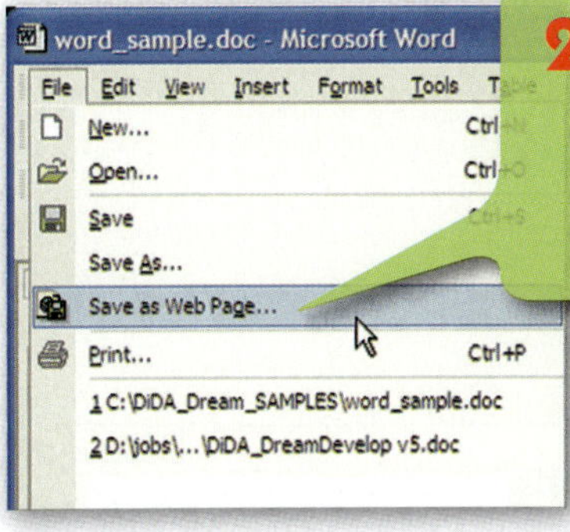

2 Select **>File >Save as Web Page**. Check that the Save as option is set to **'Web Page (*.htm) (*.html)**. Save the file in the root folder for your E-portfolio. Close the file and exit MS Word.

3 In Dreamweaver, select **>File >Open**. Select the word.htm file and choose **<Open>**.

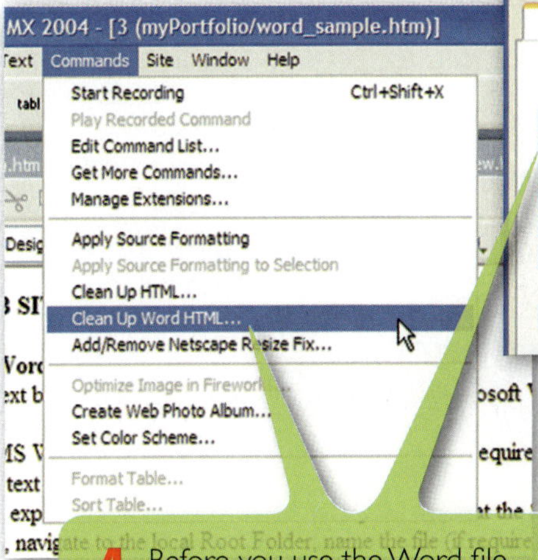

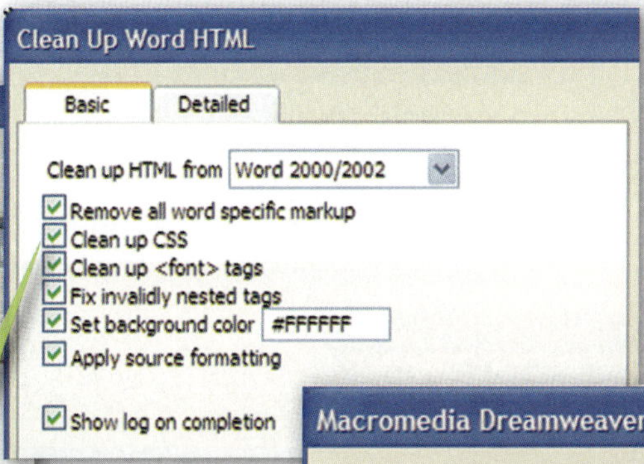

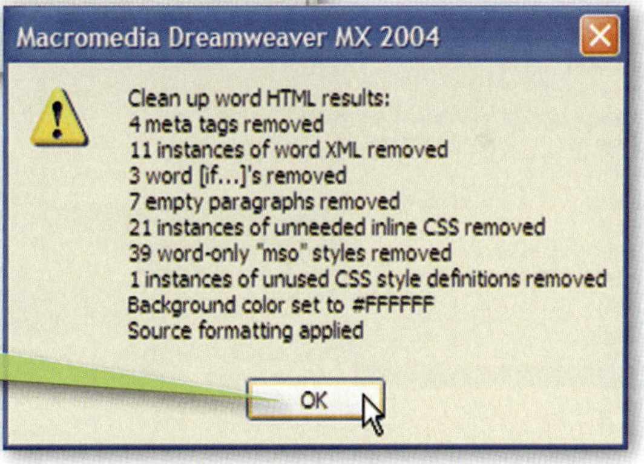

4 Before you use the Word file you need to 'clean it up'. Select **>Commands >Clean Up Word HTML** and choose **<OK >**. Select **<OK>** again when prompted.

5 Save the changes. Select all the text **(Ctrl+A)** and copy it **(Ctrl+C).**

6 Paste the text into the required region (mainContent1 in planning.htm)

7 Save the changes and preview in the browser.

! Hints and Tips !

Always make sure you save files in your Root Folder.

Import content from Excel

You will have created some spreadsheet work for your SPB to include in the E-portfolio. Sometimes you will have made screen shots of your work but you can include the spreadsheet itself if you want to.

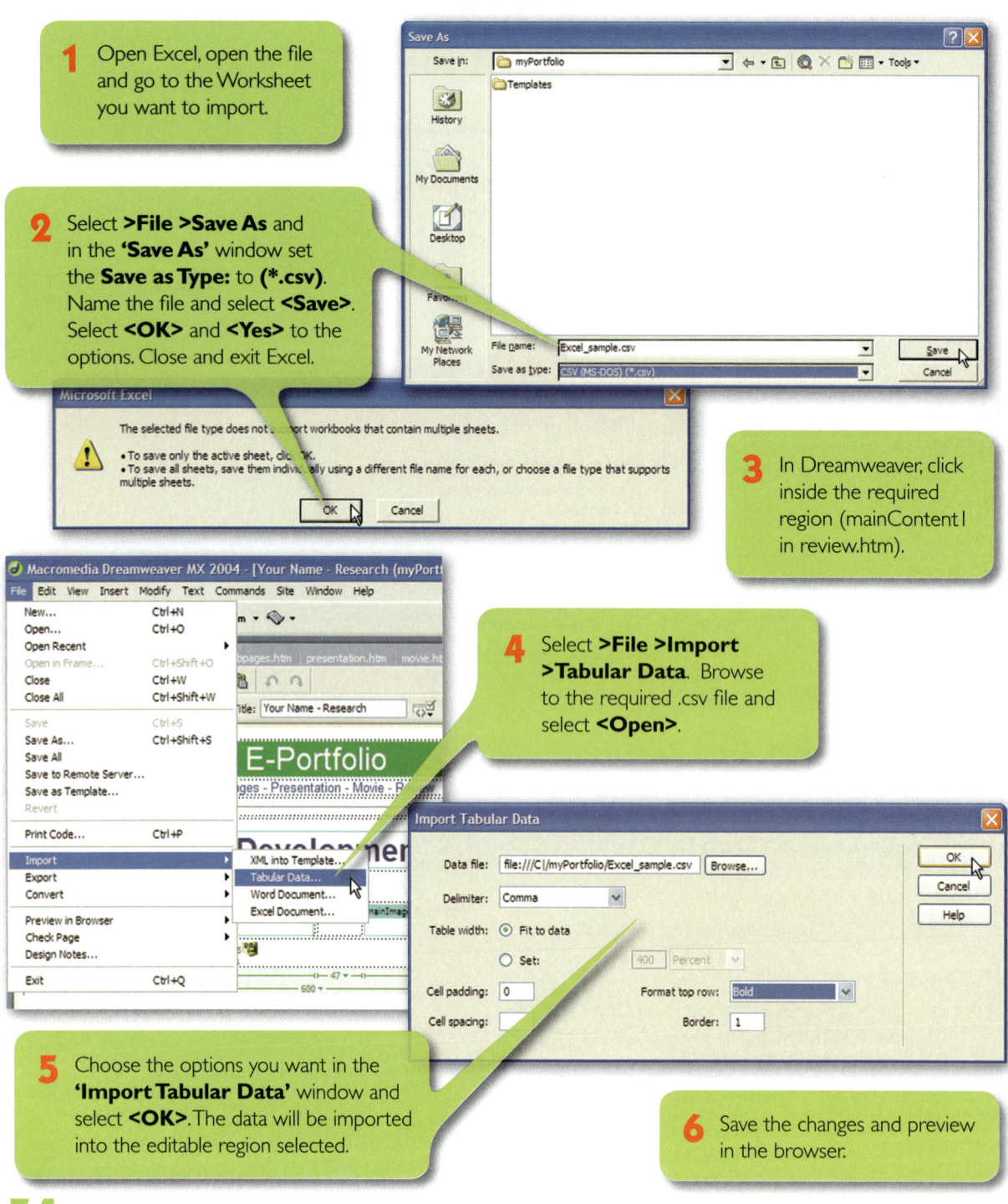

1 Open Excel, open the file and go to the Worksheet you want to import.

2 Select **>File >Save As** and in the **'Save As'** window set the **Save as Type:** to **(*.csv)**. Name the file and select **<Save>**. Select **<OK>** and **<Yes>** to the options. Close and exit Excel.

3 In Dreamweaver, click inside the required region (mainContent I in review.htm).

4 Select **>File >Import >Tabular Data**. Browse to the required .csv file and select **<Open>**.

5 Choose the options you want in the **'Import Tabular Data'** window and select **<OK>**. The data will be imported into the editable region selected.

6 Save the changes and preview in the browser.

Import a Flash file

1 Click inside the required region (mainContent2 in movie.htm).

2 Type 'Import and view a Flash asset' in the required region and press **Enter** to move the cursor to the next line down.

3 Select **>Insert >Media >Flash** from the main menu bar.

4 Navigate to a Flash movie file (.swf) and select **<OK>**.

The movie will appear as a grey rectangle with the Flash logo in the centre.

5 Select **'Autoplay'** and **'Loop'**. Play/stop the Flash movie using the controls on the Properties panel. Save the file and preview in the browser.

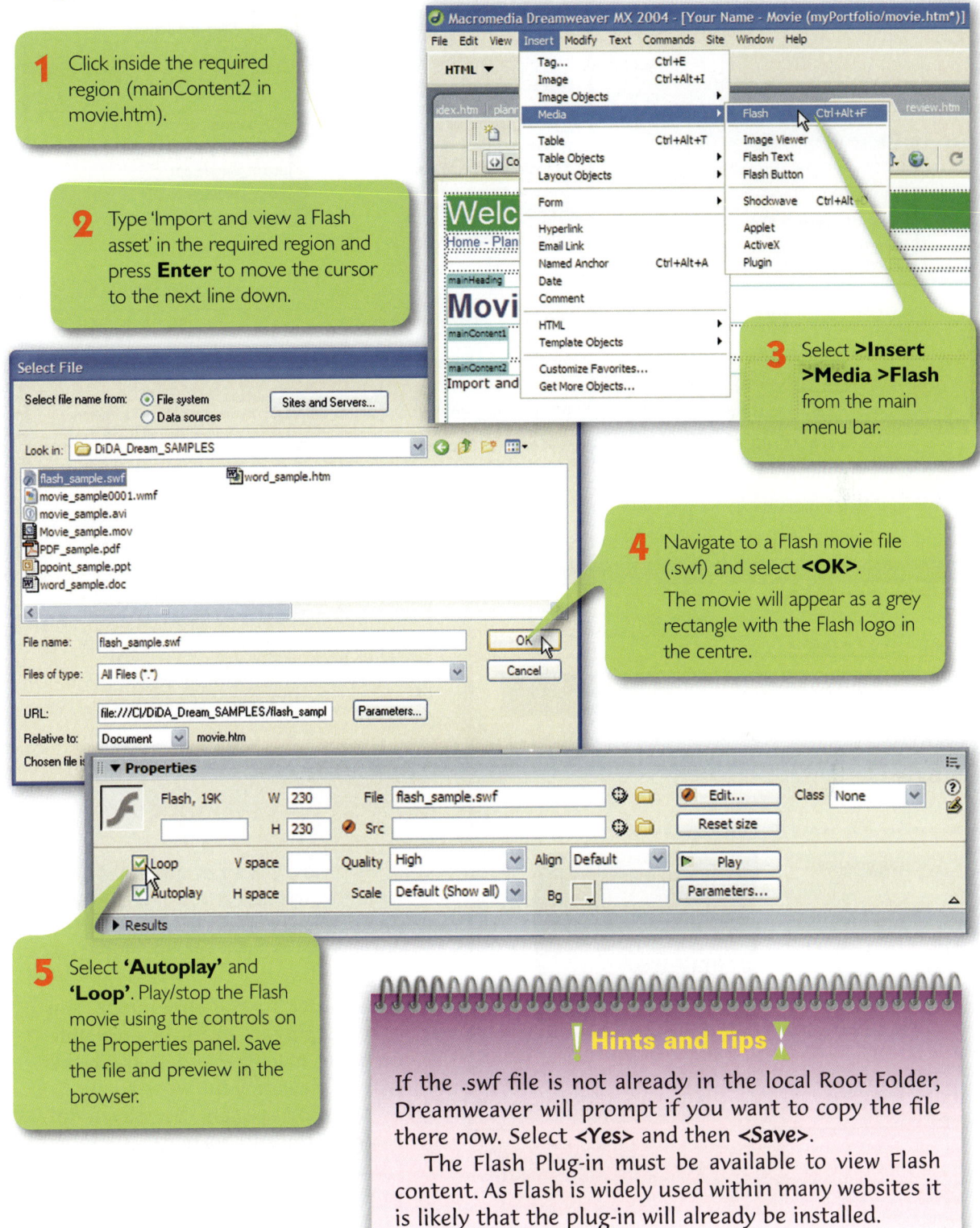

Hints and Tips

If the .swf file is not already in the local Root Folder, Dreamweaver will prompt if you want to copy the file there now. Select **<Yes>** and then **<Save>**.

The Flash Plug-in must be available to view Flash content. As Flash is widely used within many websites it is likely that the plug-in will already be installed.

Import a movie

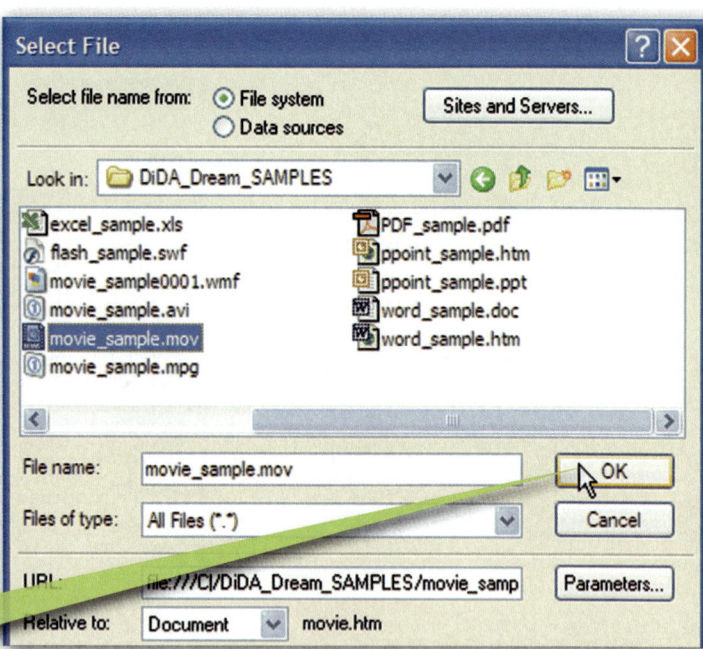

1 Click inside the required region (mainImage in movie.htm).

2 Type 'Import and view a Movie' in the required region and press **Enter** to move the cursor to the next line down.

3 Select **>Insert >Media >PlugIn** from the main menu bar.

4 Navigate to a media movie (.mov prefix) and select **<OK>**.

The movie will appear as a small grey square.

5 Play the movie from the Properties panel and resize until you can see the full image (and control bar). If your movie is not displayed within Dreamweaver, check and preview it in the browser instead.

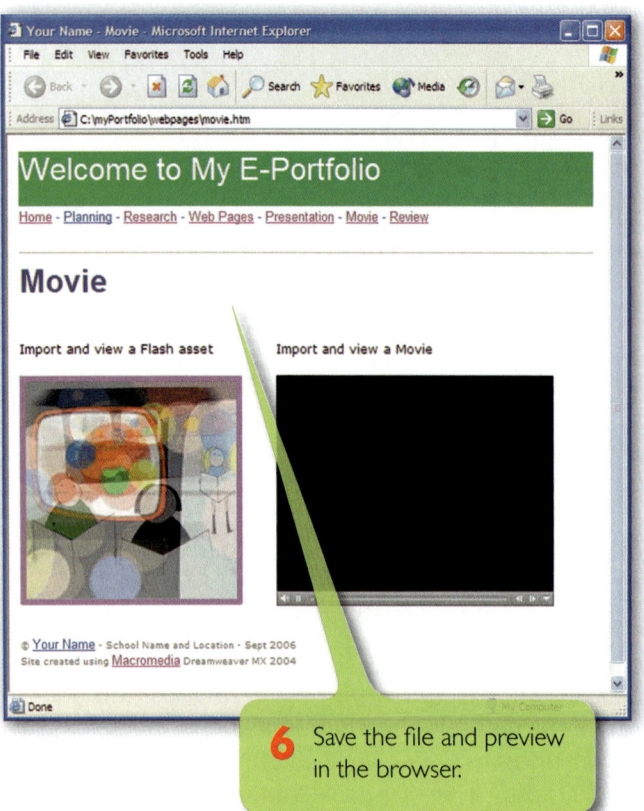

6 Save the file and preview in the browser.

! Hints and Tips

If the .mov file is not already in the local Root Folder, Dreamweaver will prompt if you want to copy the file there now. Select **<Yes>** and then **<Save>**.

In order to play any movie, the correct plug-in must be available on your machine and that of the person viewing your website.

As movies can be saved in many different formats, such as Quicktime, AVI, MPEG, it is good practice to provide more than one option.

Link to and launch a PDF file

1 Click the cursor inside the required region (mainContent2 in review.htm) and type 'Import and view a PDF File'.

2 Highlight the text.

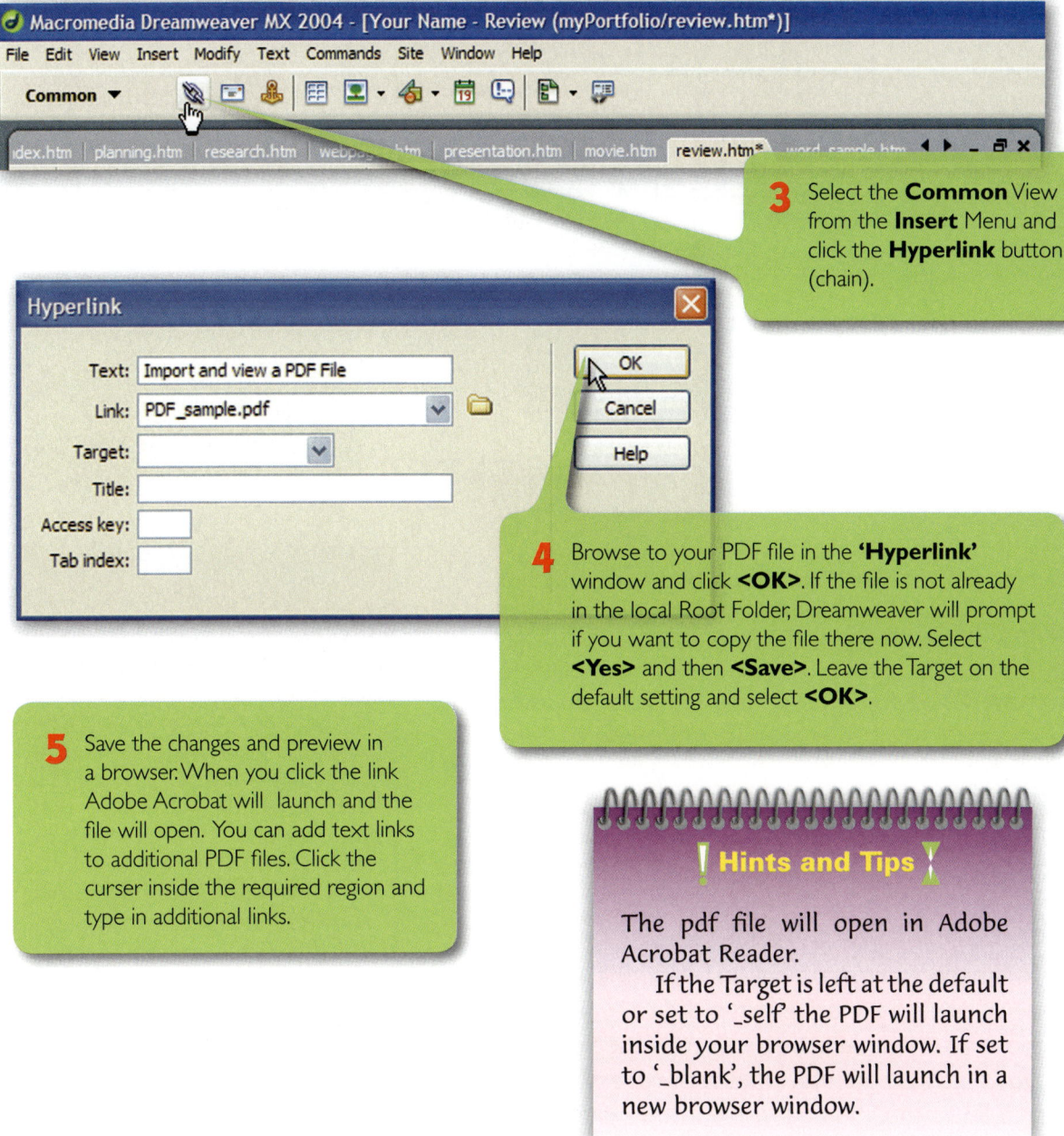

3 Select the **Common** View from the **Insert** Menu and click the **Hyperlink** button (chain).

4 Browse to your PDF file in the **'Hyperlink'** window and click **<OK>**. If the file is not already in the local Root Folder, Dreamweaver will prompt if you want to copy the file there now. Select **<Yes>** and then **<Save>**. Leave the Target on the default setting and select **<OK>**.

5 Save the changes and preview in a browser. When you click the link Adobe Acrobat will launch and the file will open. You can add text links to additional PDF files. Click the curser inside the required region and type in additional links.

! Hints and Tips

The pdf file will open in Adobe Acrobat Reader.

If the Target is left at the default or set to '_self' the PDF will launch inside your browser window. If set to '_blank', the PDF will launch in a new browser window.

Link to and launch a PowerPoint presentation

Using ICT requires you to be able to use presentation software to get your message across (see page 132 of your Student Book). The instructions show you how to add and view PowerPoint based material in your E-portfolio.

1 Open the required file in MS PowerPoint.

2 Select **>File >Save as Web Page.** Check that the Save as option is set to 'Web Page (*.htm) (*.html) and select **<Save>**.

Close the file and exit MS PowerPoint.

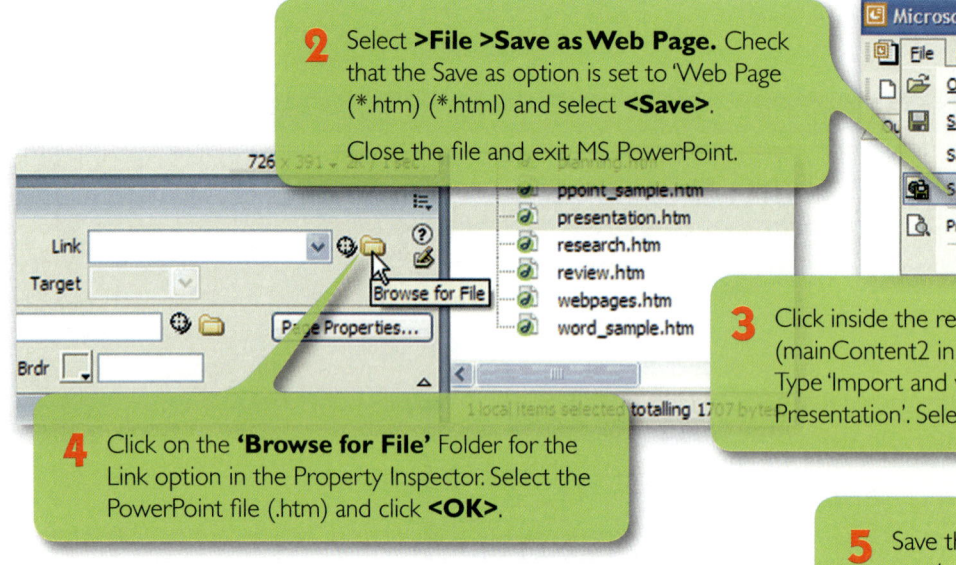

3 Click inside the required region (mainContent2 in presentation.htm). Type 'Import and view a Powerpoint Presentation'. Select and highlight this text.

4 Click on the **'Browse for File'** Folder for the Link option in the Property Inspector. Select the PowerPoint file (.htm) and click **<OK>**.

5 Save the changes and preview in the browser.

Hints and Tips

You can use the 'Browse for File' Folder to link to an actual PowerPoint file (.ppt). This will open in a different way to the .htm version. This may well be the method you will use as it opens the PowerPoint presentation in a separate window.

Link to and launch web pages

The Using ICT SPB will ask you to create web-based publications to get your message across. These pages form a website just like your E-portfolio.

You will need to create a link between the relevant page of your E-portfolio and the home page of your web pages for the SPB. Make sure that you copy the root directory for your publication into the root directory for your E-portfolio so that the links will work for your teacher and the moderator.

Hints and Tips

When you link to a publication like web pages it is very important that you test everything carefully. Open your E-portfolio web pages page in a web browser. Make sure that you can access the publication. Now check that all the links with the publication still work and that all assets on the pages are still visible and functional.

If you have a missing image, copy the original image into the right place in the root directory of the E-portfolio. If the image exists, then you may need to re-link the image.

Modify a template and update pages

Once you have imported the content, you need to test your prototype with test users. The feedback may suggest that you need to make changes to the E-portfolio.

Using templates allows you to make changes to the non-editable areas of a website quickly and easily.

Once you have made a change, Dreamweaver will offer to update all the other pages that are linked to the template.

1 Select **'main.dwt'** in the Files Panel and double-click to open it in the document window. If you can't see it you might need to click on the **'+'** button to expand the Templates folder.

2 Change the year of copyright to 2006.

3 Save the template (**>File >Save** or **Ctrl+S**).

4 Select **<Update>** when the **'Update Template Files'** window appears. This applies the changes to all the related pages.

Update Template Files

Update templates used in these files?

/webpages.htm
/index.htm
/planning.htm
/research.htm
/movie.htm
/review.htm
/presentation.htm

Update

Don't Update

Files

Files | Assets

myPortfolio | Local vie

Site - myPortfolio (C:\myPortfolio)
  ppoint_sample_files
  Templates
    main.dwt
  example.htm
  Excel_sample.csv
  flash_sample.swf

Update Pages

Look in: Files That Use... | main

Update: ☐ Library items
        ☑ Templates

Close

Help

☑ Show log   Done

Status:

updated movie.htm
updated review.htm
Done.
  files examined: 7
  files updated: 7
  files which could not be updated: 0
total time: (0:00:03)

5 The **'Update Pages'** window will show the number of files updated. When finished select **<Close>**.

6 Close the **'main.dwt'** template.

7 Open any of the pages you have created. Each page shows an * to show that unsaved changes have been made and the Copyright date has changed.

8 Click on the tab for each unsaved document and save. Use the < > arrows to help you navigate backwards and forwards.

Macromedia Dreamweaver MX 2004 - [Your Name - Presentation (myPortfolio/prese

File Edit View Insert Modify Text Commands Site Window Help

Common ▼

index.htm* | planning.htm* | research.htm* | webpages.htm* | presentation.htm* | movie.htm* | review.htm* | word_sa

Code Split Design Title: Your Name - Presentation

Detach a web page from its template

As you import content you may find that the template is not suitable for one or two of the pages you have created. You can detach the page from the template used to create it - you can then make changes to any area of the page.

1 Select and open the page in the document window.

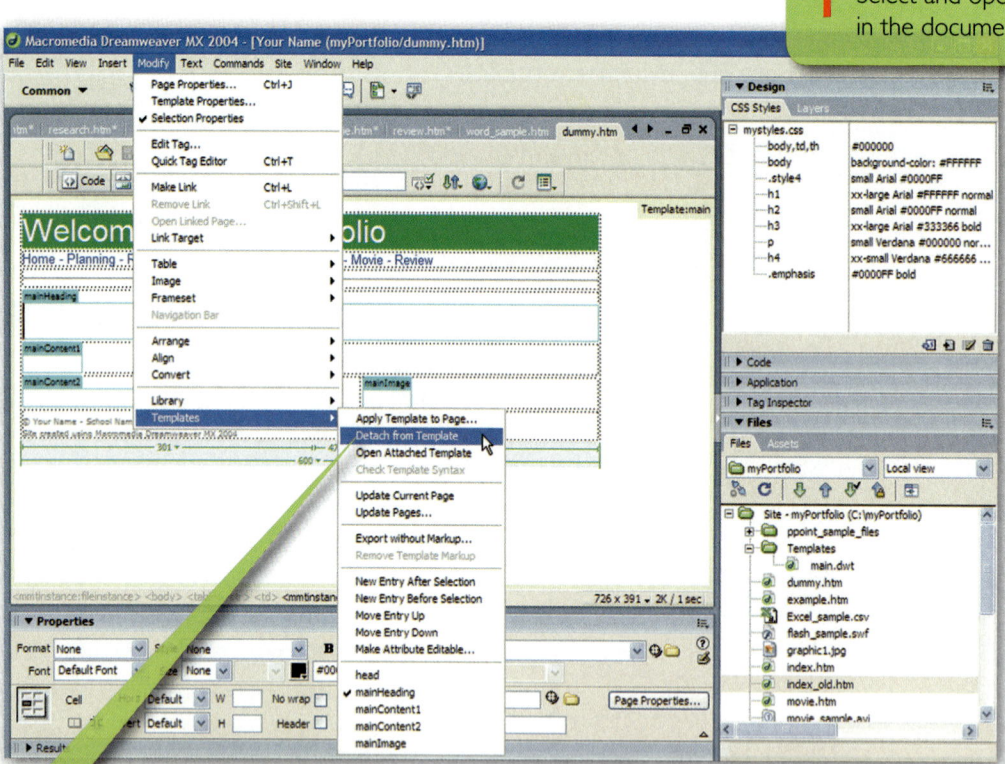

2 Check you have the right page open and select **>Modify >Templates >Detach from Template** in the main menu.

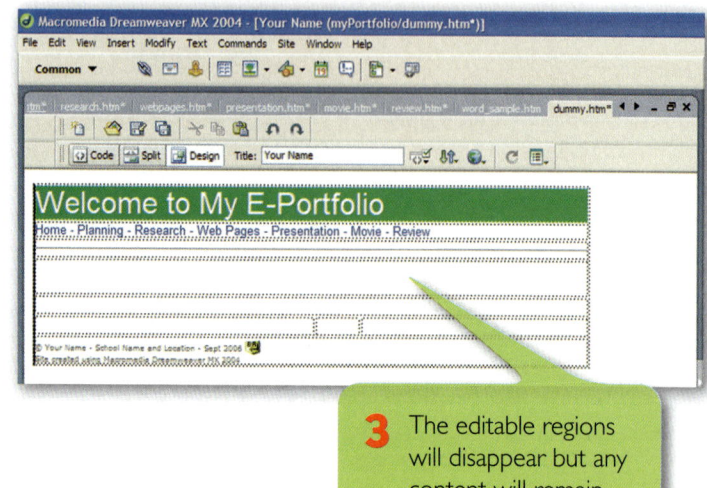

3 The editable regions will disappear but any content will remain.

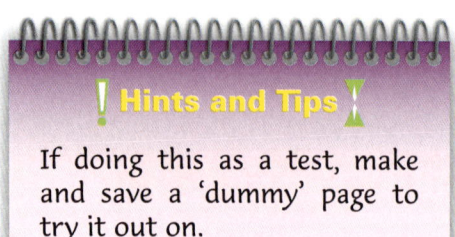

Over to you

Now that you have seen how to set up an E-portfolio you can showcase the work you have produced for your Food Matters! Project.

1 Creating templates

You created a template as part of your work for this chapter. It is important that you use a template for your E-portfolio so it is easy to use for your teacher and the moderator.
Using templates lets you create web pages that are consistent. This will mean that your teacher and the moderator know where the navigation links are and how to view your publications and evidence.

a You created some storyboards for the pages of your Food Matters! E-portfolio. Look at the designs you produced – make sure you designed them so that you can use a template to create each page. Get feedback on your designs to make sure that they are suitable for your E-portfolio.

b Create a prototype template and test it to make sure that it is suitable for your E-portfolio. Use the feedback you receive to create the template you will use for your Food Matters! E-portfolio.

c Once you have created your template, use your structure diagram to remind you which pages you need. Create, name and save the pages as you go. Make sure that your navigation system works and that all the pages are linked.

2 Import your content

a Import the notes you created for your presentation for the Year 13 students to an editable region on your presentation page.

b Import two versions of the spreadsheet work you collected onto your survey page. One version should show the results of your analysis and the other should show the formulas you used.

c Add any Flash files to your web pages.

d Import any movies to your web pages.

e Link to any PDF documents such as your formal letter or report. It is a good idea to open documents in a new browser window because it makes it much easier for your teacher and the moderator to view your documents and the supporting evidence.

f Experiment with both ways of linking to and launching the PowerPoint presentation you created for the Year 13 students. Which one is best? Which will you use when you create your real E-portfolio?

3 Link your content

a Link the web pages you created to provide information on healthy eating for parents' night. Copy your root directory for the parents' pages into the root directory for the E-portfolio before you link the pages.

b Create all the internal links you will need. It is very important that it is possible to move forwards and backwards through the pages of your E-portfolio. Your moderator is not going to be impressed if they meet a dead end.

c Create external links to any websites you used in your research and name the sources so that your teacher and the moderator can view them if they want to.

d Format the links you included in your E-portfolio.

Format the links you add as you import content into your E-portfolio or link to and launch your publications such as PDF documents and presentations and movies.

5 Completion and testing

Test a finished site

You should now have a fully functioning E-portfolio. The most important thing to do now is to test your product. You will need to get feedback from your peers, your teacher and test users to make sure that your E-portfolio is suitable for your target audience and is fit for purpose.

First check that you have entered an 'Alt Tag' for any images you have used and that you have titled each web page.

1 Close, and save all documents.

2 From the main menu bar choose **Site>Reports**...

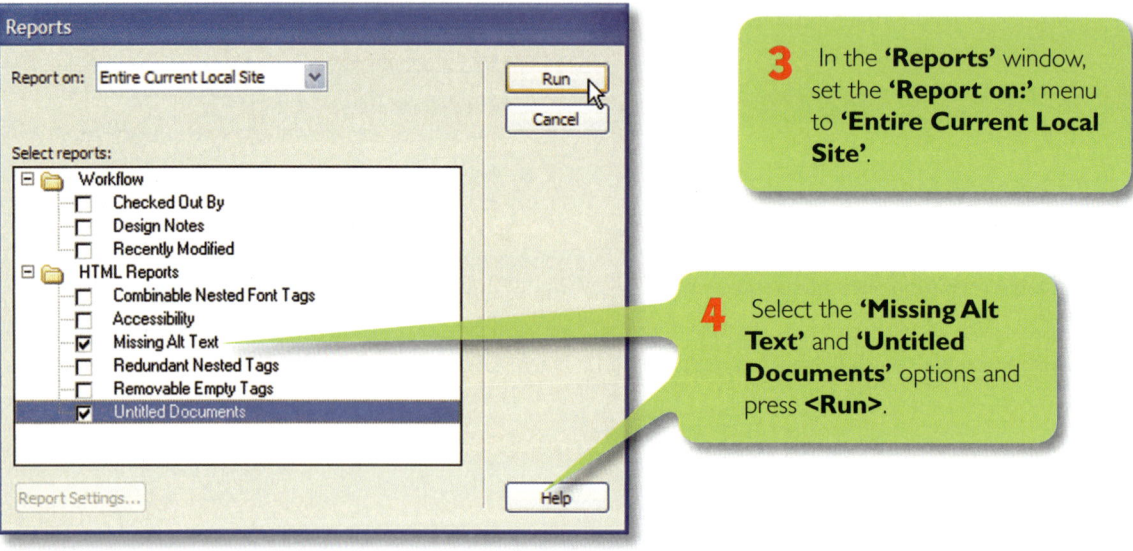

3 In the **'Reports'** window, set the **'Report on:'** menu to **'Entire Current Local Site'**.

4 Select the **'Missing Alt Text'** and **'Untitled Documents'** options and press **<Run>**.

5 The **Site report** panel should appear listing any problems for the reports chosen.

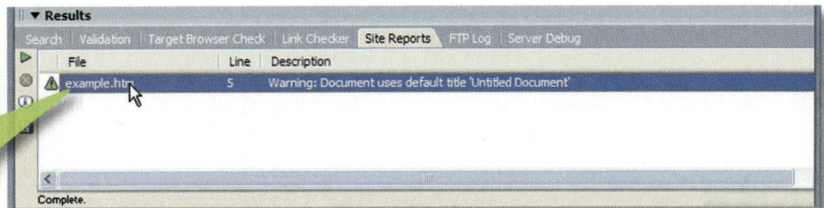

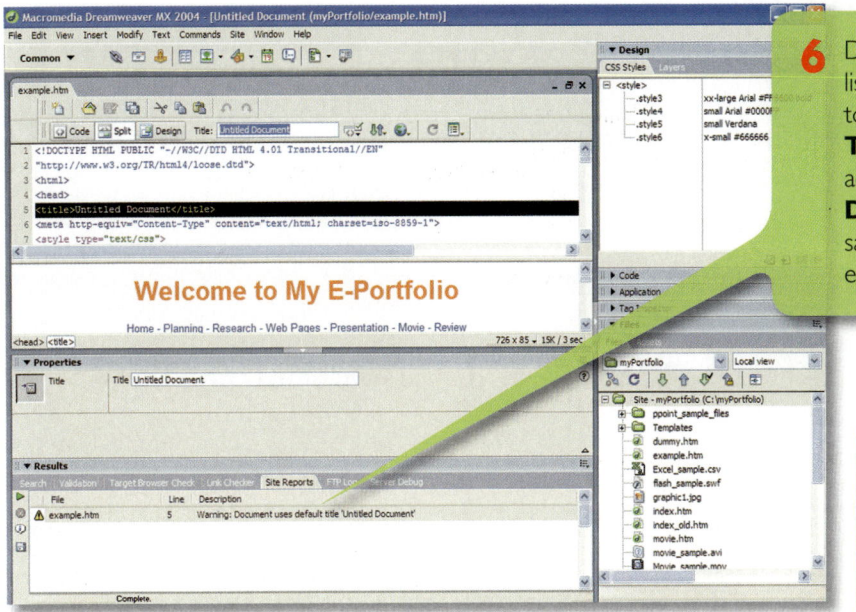

6 Double-click any documents listed in the Site Report Panel to open them. If **'Missing Alt Text'** – select the image and add a description. If **'Untitled Documents'** – then enter and save an entry in the Title field e.g. 'Your Name – Home'

7 Save and close any .htm documents that have been changed. Close the Results Panel Group.

8 Preview the finished site in a browser. Click all the links and make sure all your pages and content appear. If yes, then copy the **Local Root Folder** (with all your content) to another machine, a CD or a Flash Key. Check through it all again – running it from another machine is a good way to check you have everything!

Hints and Tips

Depending on how your site is constructed, it might look different in different browsers. If you can, it's a good idea to access your material through a variety of browsers.

Over to you

Once you have imported all the content into your Food Matters! E-portfolio you need to test your work and make sure that your E-portfolio functions properly and will work on other peoples' computers.

You can ask your peers for their opinions or ask your teacher to look at your work. The E-portfolio is aimed at an adult audience so you use other adults as your test users.

It is important to record the feedback that you receive and to use the comments to help you improve your work.

Remember it is worth 9 marks!

Maintain your E-portfolio

As you might need to further develop your site at a later date, it is useful to 'tidy up' the structure and contents of your File Panel, perhaps by creating a Folder for all your images. This will help you to locate particular files when you want to update your site (add or remove pages, change content etc).

So far, you've placed all your files in the only folder of your website – the local root folder.

As your website grows you'll find you have more and more files to maintain – webpages (.htm files), images (.jpg and .gif files), style sheets (.css files) etc.

1 In the Files panel, right-click over the local root folder at the top and choose **'New Folder'**.

2 Name the folder 'images'.

4 Create new folders and drag/drop files to organise your files and content, for example: 'webpages' (index.htm, planning.htm etc), 'styles' (mystyles.css) and 'content' (source word.htm, excel.csv etc).

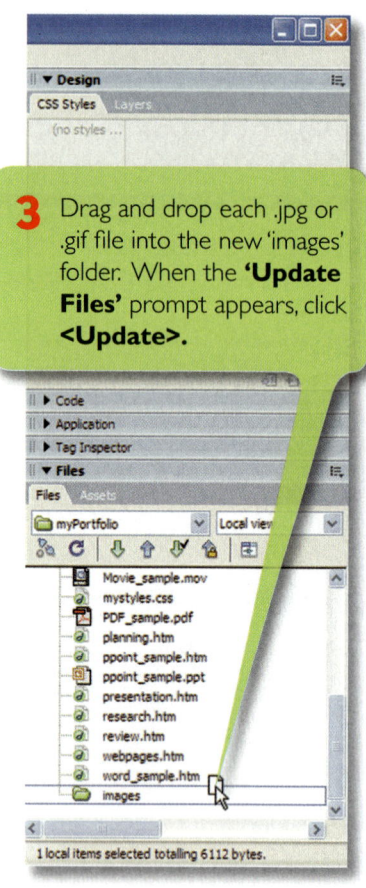

3 Drag and drop each .jpg or .gif file into the new 'images' folder. When the **'Update Files'** prompt appears, click **<Update>**.

Upload a finished site

All that stands between you and the availability of your website on the World Wide Web is a Web Server. However, as the aim of this book is to help you create an E-Portfolio, which will be run locally, this is not covered. If you wish to explore this feature further, the built in Help documentation for Dreamweaver is a great place to start. (**Main Menu Task Bar >Help**).

! Hints and Tips !

When you move or rename files or folders in the Files Panel, Dreamweaver will offer to **'Update Files'** to ensure that the references and links within the web pages continue to work. This MUST be done to ensure that your website continues to work.